Praise for
FRONTLINE MANAGEMENT EXCELLENCE

"*Front Line Management Excellence* embraces the ethics of reciprocity, often known as the Golden Rule. Dr. Watson has clearly captured how successful managers work. They treat people as they want to be treated! It certainly worked for me as I built three successful businesses, harvested them all, and found a rewarding career. A delightful read I recommend to all managers."

—John W. Altman, Serial Entrepreneur, Philanthropist

"*Frontline Management Excellence* is infused with high ideals: honesty, trustworthiness, kindness, fairness, and humility. It also stresses decisiveness and having clear expectations for quality, safety, and productivity. The idea is to balance a deep care for the people with the need to produce results. It is filled with examples of how managers produce value, develop employees, and promote better teamwork. Charlie Watson reminds us of how important it is for managers to provide people with meaning and purpose."

—Jenny Darroch, Dean, Farmer School of Business, Miami University

"From my years of experience managing research scientists in a corporate R & D laboratory in Silicon Valley, I have come to appreciate a basic principle: effective management rests on how one thinks about others and respects their feelings. It's not using pat phrases to evade real engagement. *Frontline Management Excellence* is filled with stories that demonstrate what I believe to be essential in good management, that people's feelings and emotions matter and deserve respect."

—Charles C. Morehouse, PhD

"Frontline managers are the unsung heroes of business success, weaving the threads that stitch strategy to execution. This book illuminates their pivotal role, offering a guiding light to empower and elevate every manager toward triumphant heights. A *must*-read for all new managers!"

—Jennifer Merritt, Senior Managing Director, One Workplace at Google

"Charlie Watson puts into this short, insightful book nuggets readers can use to make themselves better managers and human beings—both in the workplace and in life. While many of us may know about some of the valuable concepts covered in *Frontline Management Excellence*, having all of these delivered in an engaging, succinct manner provides a dependable pathway for managers to perform at their finest."

—Michael Keefe, Former COO for Café Nero, EasyCafe, UK; Senior Executive, Europe, Middle East and Africa Expansion for Blockbuster Video

"From anecdotal stories retold in short, bite-sized detail to practical leadership advice, Charles Watson never veers from the true north that exemplifies what it takes to lead a team: a heart for people."

—Dr. Troy Hall, Author of *Fanny Rules*

"Charles Watson's *Frontline Management Excellence* is an excellent book in management and leadership. Charles's use of storytelling helps illustrate practical ways supervisors can achieve results while building and maintaining trusting relationships."

—Dave Rowland, Author of *Green Light, Go! The Story of an Army Start-up*

"Morsels of wisdom, with a treat inside: that's what *Frontline Management Excellence* is all about. In thirty-two separate lessons, Charles Watson shares what he's experienced or heard about so that new managers can learn from his insight and stories. You must avail yourself of this knowledge, and as Charlie says in the intro, just absorb one chapter at a time. What a great way to read and put into practice key management ideas."

> —Howard H. Prager, Author of *Make Someone's Day: Becoming a Memorable Leader in Work and Life*

"It is critical that *Frontline Management Excellence* be in the hands of managers. The many narratives Charlie Watson relates provide a clear path for managers to follow as they develop trust and achieve high-quality objectives safely through participation and appreciation."

> —Peter J. Gravett, Major General, US Army (Retired), Author of *From the Ranch House to East Garrison: and Beyond* and *Battling While Black: General Patton's Heroic African-American WWII Battalions*

"*Frontline Management Excellence* presents a straightforward approach to leading others. Through examples and storytelling, this book brings concepts to life in a thoughtful and relatable manner. Dr. Watson has provided a practical handbook any manager should keep in their toolkit."

> —Regan Miller, Author of *OD for the Accidental Practitioner* and *OD for the Intentional Practitioner*

Frontline Management Excellence: Practical Methods That Produce Remarkable Results

by Charles E. Watson

© Copyright 2023 Charles E. Watson

ISBN 979-8-88824-228-5

All rights reserved. No part of this publication may be reproduced, stored in a retrieval system, or transmitted in any form or by any means—electronic, mechanical, photocopy, recording, or any other—except for brief quotations in printed reviews, without the prior written permission of the author.

Published by

◧ köehlerbooks™

3705 Shore Drive
Virginia Beach, VA 23455
800-435-4811
www.koehlerbooks.com

Note on Cover Design

The "tree" cover signifies the importance of having deep roots in a good, moral, soil. The strength of the tree is "grounded" in fertile soil of justice, ambition, forward-thinking and ability to take measured risk. Hence, the magnificent golden tree of success.

FRONTLINE MANAGEMENT EXCELLENCE

PRACTICAL METHODS THAT PRODUCE REMARKABLE RESULTS

CHARLES E. WATSON

VIRGINIA BEACH
CAPE CHARLES

In memory of my father,
James H. Watson
1907-2002

Table of Contents

Introduction 3
How to Benefit Most from This Book 5

Perspectives
1   The Work of a Manager 8
2   Make Yourself Trustworthy 11

Climates of Achievement and Satisfaction
3   Create a Climate of Congeniality 14
4   How to Earn Respect 16
5   Manage with Integrity 18
6   Treat People Right 21

Tendencies and Mindsets that Matter
7   Be a Service-Oriented Manager 24
8   Why Care About Feeling? 27
9   Have Deep Respect for People 30
10 When You Make a Mistake, Admit It 33
11 See Beyond the Obvious 36

Purpose-Driven Management Skills
12 Focus on Creating Value 40
13 Promote Quality-Mindedness 43
14 Make Your Expectations Clear 46
15 The Motivating Power of Goals 49
16 Planning for Goal Achievement 52

Leadership in Action

17	Five Ways to Inspire Employees	55
18	How Closely Should You Supervise?	60
19	Empower People to Perform	64
20	Avoid the Careless and Unthinking	67
21	Safety Practices That Work	70

Expand Employee Abilities

22	How to Orient a New Employee	75
23	How to Teach Job Skills	77
24	Improve Capabilities through Coaching	80
25	Correct with Compassion	83

Group Dynamics

26	How Group Norms Affect Behavior	86
27	The Elements of an Effective Group	89

Effective Interpersonal Communication

28	Beneath the Surface of Communication	92
29	Harness the Power of Listening	96
30	How to Be a Good Listener	99

Bringing About Improvements

31	Meet the Challenge of Change	101
32	Be the Boss You'd Like to Work For	105

About the Author	108
Let's Take the Next Step Forward	109

"Practically the entire impact of management policies falls on first-and second-level supervisors. The day-by-day interpretation and administration of policies are in their hands. Ineffective supervision makes meaningless the best policies, the best technological equipment, and the efforts of the best workers."

—Milton M. Mandell

Introduction

FRONTLINE MANAGERS PERFORM a vital function in business and industry. Their unit's productivity, quality, morale, and safety depend on their skills and abilities. These action-oriented persons are hungry for practical ideas and methods to help them perform more effectively. They want a reliable resource that is (1) brief and to the point, (2) practical, easy to read, and filled with actual examples, and (3) focused on how to bring out the best in others.

Frontline Management Excellence depicts incidents from the work lives of managers and supervisors. It shows what they did and the consequences that followed. Unlike textbooks, with explanations of theories that are usually soon forgotten, this book is filled with stories that will be long remembered. These stories will empower readers with more than knowledge of effective management practices. The concrete examples I cite will supply readers with the thought, *I understand what the story taught me. I now know what to do. And I want to use that idea myself.* Of course, all situations are different. Thus, the lessons readers learn will require cleverness to modify the principles gained to fit their unique circumstances.

Good management is not a bag of tricks used to get something wanted. There is more to it than merely applying time-tested methods. The manager's character as a person needs to be considered. What are the manager's motives, deep-seated feelings, and attitudes toward others? Does the manager live by high ideals, such as kindness, integrity, sincerity, and decency? Or is the manager little more than a small-minded manipulator? Phonies do not fool people. They want to contribute to worthwhile purposes, feel they matter as people, and know that their work matters. They will do their best to please authentic, honorable bosses. This is why a manager's integrity is vitally important.

Stories of persons living by high ideals, like that of the Good Samaritan, teach a lesson and something more. They convey inspiring models that prompt our inner voice to urge us to live in admirable ways ourselves. The examples of managers depicted herein acting honorably and humanely will cause readers to think, *I want to become more like that respectable person.*

Lastly, I suggest you work closely with your organization's human resources department and follow their advice. You'll be glad you did.

How to Benefit Most from This Book

IN THE FIRST minutes of a management training course I once conducted, an attendee confronted me with a challenging question. "Are you here," he asked, "to tell us how to do our jobs?" From the body language and expressions on the faces of those there, I knew his question was rehearsed and on the minds of others in the room.

It's always a good idea to be honest and respectful. Seeing situations from the perspective of others is a solid step toward earning trust. I realized that sitting before me was a group of experienced foremen. They had seen a lot in their work lives and were rightfully skeptical of me, an unknown outsider. Who was I to be so presumptuous as to tell them how to do their jobs? They deserved more than a simple "no" to their loaded question. These were practical people who didn't want to sit passively and listen. They wanted to learn by doing. I realized the smart thing to do was demonstrate that I understood their feelings. I told the group, "You don't know me, and I don't know you. I know little about what you do and those you supervise. I'm not here to tell you how to do your jobs because effective management isn't learned by listening. It's learned by doing. It's learned by working for or alongside other managers, seeing what they did that proved successful and what did not. We will examine real situations to help you develop the skills of observation, insight, and analysis. We will learn what worked out well or poorly for other managers."

You can learn significantly from competent managers who get things right and incompetent ones who don't. *Frontline Management Excellence* does not tell readers how to manage. Instead, it presents valuable frameworks to help them better understand situations and decide which courses of action are most apt to produce desired outcomes. Remember, your quest to become a better manager involves developing the skills of insight, analysis, and judgment. Think of the examples and methods described herein as being a fountain of valuable concepts and frameworks that you can use to sharpen your insight, deepen your analyses, and improve your decision-making abilities. Notice how successful managers size up situations, analyze what is happening, and decide what to do.

The best way to get the most value from this book is to become an active learner. This means thinking about what you have just read and allowing your mind to digest it more thoroughly. It would be best if you read the book slowly. Reading large chunks of it speedily might make you aware of many ideas. But it won't allow you to think deeply and see many hidden nuances and implications of what was written. My suggestion is this: read one chapter at a sitting. Then, put the book aside for a day and consider what you read. Give your mind some time to mull over the ideas covered. Ask yourself, "What went on in the examples depicted? What happened as a result? What lessons can I learn from these events?" You'll be surprised by the workings of your mind and what it comes up with in the way of insights. You will arrive at conclusions that make sense and are believable because you have thought them out through and through yourself.

Next, think about the attitudes, mindsets, and tendencies that underlie the actions of the managers depicted in the stories you read. Ask yourself, "Do I have the same feelings, attitudes, and thinking patterns? Might I be more effective if I change how I think about others and the situations I find myself in?"

Finally, develop creative ways of adapting the general principles learned to meet your unique circumstances. Use your imagination. Assess what worked well and what went wrong. Try to learn from your experiences. Check out your ideas with others. Keep your mind alive and growing. Reread selected chapters as you see fit. It helps to have a positive, can-do attitude.

Realize that some of the topics covered here might apply to something other than your specific duties and responsibilities. Pick out what you can use and put these ideas to work. Positive-minded readers who eagerly seek new ideas and better methods will find them and put them to good use. And, too, readers who wish to search for things to scoff at won't be disappointed by their quests either.

1

The Work of a Manager

RONALD WAS A first-rate diesel mechanic, and his coworkers looked up to him. Management saw this and decided to promote Ronald to a supervisory position. He would now be responsible for scheduling work, training new mechanics, supervising crew members, and evaluating their performance. It was a role that required communicating, organizing, motivating, and training skills.

Ronald tried his best to comply with his boss's suggestions for organizing and supervising those under him. But after a short while, Ronald was back on the shop floor, doing the work himself. Whenever his boss questioned him about spending too much time doing work instead of training and supervising, Ronald answered, "This is a tough repair job, and I'm the only one who knows how to handle it."

Ronald wasn't cut out to be a manager because he didn't care about encouraging and developing the abilities of the other mechanics. He was interested in one thing only—repairing machinery himself. There are thousands of intelligent, clever, hardworking, responsible individuals. Pay them a fair day's wage, and they will give an honest day's work. But don't assume everyone has what it takes to be a manager. If you want to find effective managers, look for individuals with a sincere interest in developing the know-how and skills of others. If they don't genuinely care about those they manage, they will be unable to excite people's loyalty, enthusiasm, cooperation, and efforts.

Managing involves guiding and inspiring others to produce quality goods and services. It also consists of cultivating better, capable, dedicated, motivated, talented, cooperative, and enthusiastic employees. Turning out abundant high-quality work is one part of the manager's job. The other part is to create more valuable employees. This requires a sincere interest in others and the ability to train and develop their talents.

One more thing: today's workplaces require employees to work in groups. Cooperation isn't just a nicety; it's a necessity. People need to communicate better and work alongside each other better despite their differences in backgrounds, social status, and beliefs. Teamwork is necessary for identifying problems, diagnosing causes, and implementing agreed-upon solutions. Today's managers need to develop workplaces that provide people with a sense of belonging, accomplishment, and fulfillment from using their ideas and efforts and working with others.

To summarize, the work of a manager is (1) to produce value, (2) to develop employee abilities, and (3) to promote better teamwork. Excellent managers focus on making continual improvements in these three areas. Effective competitors always find places for improvement. Imagine a sports team that just finished a game and performed well. In the future, an excellent coach will discover ways to make their team's players even more fit and talented, with better teamwork skills.

What do managers do? What functions do they perform? The list is long: goal setting, planning, organizing, controlling, evaluating performance, motivating, communicating, training, leading, implementing change, making decisions, solving problems, etc.

Some management functions deal with tangible, logical, and measurable issues. These include goal setting, planning, organizing, evaluating, inspecting, and controlling. These are called the *structural forces* of management. These functions provide purpose, direction, and stability.

But a logical, rigid framework, like a skeleton, cannot do anything alone. It is lifeless. The *activating forces* of managing are needed to breathe life into organizations. These management functions include leading, communicating, training, motivating, and coaching. *Activating forces* excite men and women to be creative, cooperative, and committed team players.

Managers must be skillful at using structural and activating forces to be effective. Additionally, they must be equally concerned with production and people matters. The most effective managers give as much attention to achieving tangible output, in terms of quantity and quality, as they do to attending to the feelings and well-being of the producers who cause the result. Buildings, machinery, equipment, materials, and money are all needed and used in business, but they cannot produce independently; they need people for that. The living, breathing people put life into a business and cause it to build, grow, and prosper.

2
Make Yourself Trustworthy

IT'S NORMAL FOR new managers to have questions like these: Will my people perform as I want? Will they respect me? Will they help me succeed? Will they work hard? Will they do their jobs correctly? Can I trust them? Overconcern for these sorts of worries will put you on the wrong path.

My advice is to look at the situation from the other side. Instead, imagine the questions your subordinates will likely have about you:

Will our new supervisor be fair?

Will she respect me?

Will he value my contributions?

Will we get along?

Will I like working for this person?

Can I trust the new boss?

The best way to create favorable relationships with others is to be trustworthy. Trust is one of the most valuable attributes a person can earn, especially those who manage others. Trust makes sound and satisfying relationships possible. Friendships, marriages, families, work groups, and enterprises depend on it. If your employees don't trust you, they certainly won't give their best efforts. People will tolerate an occasional out-of-character bust of anger from a boss. They will forgive mistakes and cases of bad judgment from time to time. But human nature is so organized that untrustworthiness is unacceptable. It has ruined friendships and marriages, crippled organizations, and even brought on the collapse of governments. In discussing the idea of trust, one man told me, "If I can't trust an individual, then I don't want to work with him."

Surveys that ask respondents to identify the qualities of a lousy leader find "bad-mouths others behind their backs" and "betrays trust" near the top of the list. Untrustworthiness reveals itself, very often, in little things: twisting rules to favor self, not being utterly aboveboard in dealings, hedging on ethical standards—if one cannot get what's wanted fairly and honestly, then it's okay to obtain it sneakily, provided no one will ever know. Regardless, sooner or later, the truth always comes out.

Distrust is frequently caused by the unwillingness to honestly face one's destructive tendencies, mistakes, and shortcomings. For example, a manager fails an assignment because it was inadequately planned. Materials did not arrive in time because they were ordered too late. Trying to avoid blame, the manager claims the snafu was the fault of lazy employees. This leads to resentment and causes some people to quit while others stay and become bitter and less productive.

Blaming one's circumstances for failures is another way people can destroy trust. For example, in an emotion-filled meeting, someone makes unkind and hurtful remarks to another person. Rather than admitting to being uncivil and out of line, this person refuses to apologize and blames the angry outburst on the tension of the meeting, saying, "You made me so angry, I couldn't help it."

The best way to earn trust is through obedience to humanistic and ethical ideals. A man named Israel Cohen began his grocery business in Washington, DC. It flourished because he set an excellent example for his employees. In time, his Giant Food grocery stores grew to be among the largest chains in the country.

Mr. Cohen would frequently go to the dairy section in his store, pick up several fresh eggs, and conspicuously pay for them at the checkout lane, as would any customer. He would take his purchase to a nearby café, where the cook would make egg salad sandwiches for Mr. Cohen's noontime meal. A young lad named Charles Lazarus (who later founded and ran Toys "R" Us) worked for Mr. Cohen and would sometimes join him. The young boy was puzzled by his boss's practice. He asked, "Mr. Cohen, why did you buy those eggs? They're yours." Cohen answered, "That's exactly why I bought them. Everyone should see that everything that goes out of this store gets paid for."

Trustworthy managers reveal themselves by what they refuse to tolerate and by what they insist happens in their units. Here are examples of this quality:

A conscientious and highly productive employee with a superior attitude once tried to tell her supervisor about two coworkers who came to work late and then took an extended lunch break. The supervisor refused to listen and told the tattletale to mind her business.

An introverted person, dubbed "the nerd" behind his back, has well-reasoned thoughts about how the work unit should handle a difficult situation. The manager, who treats everyone evenhandedly, insists that all ideas and suggestions will be listened to respectfully and considered based on their merits, not on the popularity of the person making them.

3
Create a Climate of Congeniality

THE BEST WORKPLACES are usually marked by an upbeat, friendly atmosphere where people like working with each other, believe in what they are doing, and are highly confident they'll succeed together, come what may. If their boss is cheerful, helpful, upbeat, and success-focused, workers tend to think and act in these ways, too.

When I was young, a family moved to a town near our home. The Caylors came to open and run a neighborhood grocery store. They were exceedingly cheerful and outgoing. Their friendliness was genuine; it was who they were. Their business, Model Market, opened, and soon, shoppers began flocking there to buy groceries. Shoppers came because the store had something else: an unusually friendly atmosphere. It was a happy place where people were greeted with a smile and cheerful chitchat. Bag boys offered to carry groceries out to your car. If you happened to enter the store in a sour mood, you were likely to leave in a better frame of mind, uplifted by the sunny, upbeat attitudes you encountered. The friendly nature of the Caylors seemed to rub off on their store's employees. They, in turn, treated each other and customers the same way. The atmosphere of friendliness enticed shoppers into Model Market, partly to purchase wanted groceries and to be uplifted by the cheerfulness of those who worked there.

Attitudes and dispositions are contagious. Positive, cheerful leaders tend to evoke similar attitudes in their followers, whereas nasty, sour, backbiting sorts bring out like qualities in those under their authority. A positive mood on the part of leaders suggests faith in the future that things will turn out agreeably. There may be bumps in the road ahead, but these will be overcome. Genuine cheerfulness is attractive. People are drawn to it; they tend to go out of their way to encounter cheerful sorts. Cheerful moods boost morale. They also cause people to be more cooperative, productive, and optimistic about what they do.

> *Set a good example of positivity and friendliness. Live by an upbeat, can-do attitude. Believe and act in ways that convey confidence in your people and their success.*

4
How to Earn Respect

SHORTLY AFTER GRADUATING from high school, I got a job at a local factory, where I worked in the grinding department on the swing shift. My duties involved removing burrs from castings of electric can opener housings. My boss was a man named Victor. I liked him. He was pleasant. He told me what to do and how to do it in nice ways.

One afternoon before work started, Victor approached me, holding a stack of photographs. "Look at these," he said.

I asked, "Are these of your family?"

"No!" he quickly shot back with disgust.

He began showing the pictures. The first was of two men knocking at the door of a house. The next photo was of two women welcoming the men inside. The third picture was of the four people drinking beer. The next shot had them kissing and starting to remove their clothing. At that point, I told Victor, "I don't want to see any more of your pictures." I walked away. Even at seventeen, I had a fair idea of the other pictures. This incident tarnished my opinion of Victor. I steered clear of him as best I could.

When the people in personnel realized that I was not yet eighteen years of age, they put me on the day shift, which meant I had a different boss, Rocco. His demeanor was serious, all business. He was the boss, and he didn't try to be my friend.

I was nearby when Rocco told a man that he spent a Sunday afternoon making tomato paste with his wife. Hearing this made me think of him as a family man concerned with wholesome activities.

This, I respected.

One day, Rocco asked me if I would come two hours early to work overtime. I did. Then, on the following morning, I arrived early again. About fifteen minutes before the regular starting time, Rocco showed up. He seemed to be surprised to see me working. He asked, "What are you doing here?"

I said, "You asked me to come early."

"No, no," he said. "That was just for yesterday." Then he shrugged his shoulders and said, "I can understand that. I guess I didn't make it clear what I wanted. It's okay." I realized my error and was glad that Rocco understood my mistake. It felt safe to work for him; he was a good boss.

> *The best way to earn respect is to respect others, their talents, and their contributions. Act in decent, respectable, upstanding ways. Be friendly, but don't try to be friends with your subordinates. Make a point to treat everyone equitably.*

5
Manage with Integrity

SOME EXAMPLES SHOW it is smart to operate in a highly ethical fashion. When you manage with integrity, your unit will perform better, and everyone will take incredible pride in their work. And, too, everyone will have a clear conscience and sleep better at night because of it.

In a newspaper column, Hugh Aaron, in Belfast, Maine, described what happened when he ran his business with integrity. From his association with his father's upholstering business, Hugh grew up knowing how easy it is for a vendor to cheat a customer. The customer couldn't see the quality of materials hidden beneath the cover of an overstuffed chair. Hugh's father lived by a higher standard, always giving customers fair value, even though many of his competitors did not.

With knowledge of these practices, Hugh Aaron became skeptical of honesty in business. His concerns served him well when, years later, he became an entrepreneur, making color concentrates for the plastics industry. In that business, Hugh knew he could get away with using cheaper pigments or offgrade plastic matrixes. But he didn't. Occasional mistakes and omissions would occur in billings—a supplier would forget to send a bill for materials shipped, or a vendor might have billed too little or not at all. These temptations showed up from time to time. But Hugh was not going to be corrupted. He refused to take the easy path for quick gains or rationalize wrongdoing with the frequently heard excuse, "Everyone else is doing it." Rather than take advantage of these situations by remaining silent, Hugh Aaron instructed his staff to inform the parties of their errors, and his employees eagerly did so.

In Hugh's business, there were no under-the-table payments, no free vacations, no nights on the town, no bedroom companions—none of these things. The company was conducted strictly on business terms, and it worked well. His business performed far better than if he had operated on less stringent standards.

Hugh's highly moral approach to business caused employees to take pride in their organization because they could take pride in themselves. Policies grounded in simple honesty created a feeling of mutual trust. Many of his employees liked working for a "straight" company. Hugh was not a leader who would tell employees he couldn't afford this or that and then go out and buy himself an overpriced luxury car. He compensated fairly the rank-and-file employees who made his company successful. There wasn't greed at the top, and there wasn't a union to protect the folks at the bottom. Other benefits from this moral approach followed. Customers remained loyal, and vendors handled Hugh's production needs and other requests. His firm became known as a company of integrity. Consequently, morale rocketed, productivity improved, and customers felt well served. And sales and profits kept climbing.

◻◻◻

I once spent a day with Bill Huessong—vice president of manufacturing for Shopsmith Inc. in Dayton, Ohio, at the time. Many people are familiar with the Shopsmith name. The company makes a five-in-one power woodworking tool. Bill told me something important about his company's president, John Folkerth. He said, "With John, there isn't any room for gray in matters of right and wrong. To him, it's either black or white; things are right or wrong."

Consequently, everyone working for John knew that certain things would be tolerated, and others would not. This climate gave everyone at Shopsmith Inc. a clear understanding of boundaries and acceptable behavior.

John got wind that a few people in his organization installed a computer software program on more than one of the company's computers. They bought one copy of the software and installed it on multiple computers—violating the copyright agreement. Mr. Folkerth immediately put a stop to it. He ordered his purchasing department to pay the software publisher for what they were using, just as the agreement stipulated. One person involved offered *the* excuse—"But that's what everyone else does." Mr. Folkerth was unimpressed and unmoved. He told the employee, "We don't do that here. We pay for what we use."

> *Honesty pays. It attracts better talent. It produces better quality results. And it assures higher levels of commitment from everyone. It is less stressful to tell the truth, and you'll sleep better knowing you did the right thing.*

6
Treat People Right

AN EMPLOYEE OF United Parcel Service once recalled a telling incident that revealed how that company's founder and chair, Jim Casey, regarded people: "We were reviewing plans for a sorting facility to be located in the basement of one of our buildings. Jim, after listening to a complete review of the plans, asked, 'How about the ventilation for the people who will be working down there?' His first thought was for the people."

Does the manager think of humans as just another resource to be used as needed? Or does the manager treat others with respect and care? Here are examples of successful leaders who "got it right."

Once, in Chicago, a man named Paul Galvin had an idea—and he made it work. He developed a radio that could operate in an automobile. His company, Motorola, prospered because of it. Paul had definite ideas on how to treat those who built his radios. While visiting one of his plants, Paul noticed a group of women working on a production line. That wasn't unusual, but these women were bundled up in overcoats to keep out of the cold. Paul asked the shop foreman, "Why?" The answer: because they were running production on a single line, and the remainder of the shop was idle. They were cutting costs by conserving fuel and heat.

Paul Galvin reacted sternly. "I don't care if one woman is working, ten, or one hundred. You treat them alike and don't save money by abusing anyone."

In Western culture, we have inherited an ethic that has steadily elevated the quality of life. Humans, we believe, are not to be used for the service of things; things are to be used for the benefit of humans. The story that follows from David McCullough's book, *The Path Between the Seas*, illustrates treating people as they ought to be treated.

In 1905, John Stevens went to Panama. His assignment was to build a canal. Years earlier, the French had tried and failed. The technology and science of the day were inadequate to meet the challenges, and the costs were too great for private financing. Panama was a death trap; malaria, yellow fever, typhoid, intestinal disease, and pneumonia made working there impossible. After a year's effort, the United States was about to give up on the idea altogether.

President Roosevelt turned to Stevens—a railroad construction engineer and frontiersman. Once there, Stevens saw the difficulty immediately. Food prices were unaffordable. Some men foraged to survive. Living conditions were despicable—sanitation practically nonexistent, smells and filth everywhere. Men felt trapped in this tropical wilderness. A canal would be built, Stevens told them, but first things first.

Panama City and Colon must be cleaned up. Work crews dug sewers. They paved streets and sidewalks. They built commissaries, mess halls, barracks, cold-storage facilities, schools, churches, laundries, reservoirs—entire communities. Cities were fumigated, cisterns and cesspools were oiled weekly, brush was cleared, swamps and marshes were drained, water was piped, and sanitary cups were provided. It was the most extensive cleanup and health campaign ever undertaken.

Workers had fresh eggs, lettuce, and ice for the first time. Bakeries turned out fresh bread. The Isthmus of Panama was rid of the dreaded yellow fever. First things came first—before the digging.

❑❑❑

In any human enterprise, success happens only when workers believe people at the top care and are looking out for their welfare. William S. Anderson, who once ran NCR—transforming it from a firm that made mechanical cash registers to a leader in producing ATMs and store self-checkout devices—once told me, "I think the average employee wants his boss to care for him. He might like the company he works for and is happy about his work. But if he thinks his boss treats him just as another piece on a chessboard, that he's just a number, even though the boss calls him by his first name, he's not likely to be as happy, hardworking, and loyal as he could be. But if he thought, *My boss is interested in me as a person. He likes me. He asks about my wife. He knows about my kids and what they do. He knows about our family's health, even something about our dog. Therefore, he's interested in me as a human being* . . . the average person wants that. And, if he believes that you have his interest at heart, he'll also have your interest at heart." Good leaders sincerely care how people feel, especially about their work and their coworkers.

> *The best measure of what and who you are as a human being is how you think about and treat others. An excellent way to earn employees' trust and willingness to work is to treat them like human beings. Remember, things exist to be used; people live to be loved. This means treating them well by developing their abilities and rewarding their contributions.*

7

Be a Service-Oriented Manager

EISENHOWER'S BIOGRAPHER, STEPHEN Ambrose, recounted a meaningful incident. It occurred when the general came upon a group of junior officers eating their meal while their enlisted men were still waiting for theirs. Ike scolded them, saying, "You are not to eat until you've seen that your men are fed first."

Accomplishments, promotions, and new titles carry the risk of a swelled ego. Some people might feel entitled to extra privileges and special treatment when this occurs. Worse yet, they lose sight of their obligations and what their new responsibilities might allow them to do.

The only way to avoid the trap of self-importance is by serving some worthy end. To avoid doing wrong, replace your destructive impulses with good ones. Forget yourself and trying to gain more status and recognition. Instead, see to it that those you manage are treated well and productive and proficient in what they do. Find ways to make your workplace safer, more effective, and more enjoyable—where people will thrive.

In *Our Partnership Legacy,* United Parcel Service founder and CEO Jim Casey recounted an incident when a sizable contingent of managers stayed at a motel. Day and night, they were preparing for hearings on an application for interstate operative rights. The meeting room was chilly and drafty. One of the men felt his throat grow scratchy and worried about getting a cold. Concerned that a sore throat and sniffles could hurt his part of the presentation, the man asked whether anyone had cough drops, but no one did. Casey was in the room at the time. Moments later, he disappeared. An hour later, the chairman returned with several packages of cough drops. He had quietly slipped away and walked a mile along the main highway to the nearest store. It was Casey's attitude that if there were a way he could help, he should. He said, "If cough drops help, and I can get them, I ought to be the one."

It's a mistake to think too highly of yourself and try to get others to go along with that—because they won't. Instead, be your authentic self. Authenticity goes a long way in earning credibility with others, particularly those who work for and alongside you. Don't take yourself too seriously. This means being the person you are, not some arrogant big shot. Think of managing in terms of serving. View your role as a privilege, and you will get along with others and perform work better.

Mike Wright, CEO of Super Valu Stores, once told me, "Whether you are a teacher, business executive, or priest, you should worry about whether your ego has gotten out of control. I think more problems result from an ego imbalance than anything else. You've always got to ask yourself, *What am I doing to be a jerk around here?*

Jack Sparks, who ran Whirlpool then, once mentioned what he advises managers: "Don't try to be something you're not. People will spot you if you try."

❑❑❑

The most successful, high-level managers I've come across offer this advice to those on their way up: You cannot be successful entirely through your own efforts. If you are to accomplish anything worthwhile, you'll do it only through the help and cooperation of others.

When he was a young man working for Johnson & Higgins of California, the insurance brokerage firm, Dick Ross had an outstanding year. That December, top management told Dick he would receive a nice bonus. Most young people would immediately visualize how such a windfall might be used, especially with a young family at

Christmastime. But Dick Ross didn't do that. Instead, he told top management that he didn't feel he could accept the entire bonus himself because, although he had some success, it was mainly due to the team of people that gave him backup to get the job done. The only way he would accept the bonus would be if it were shared with the group. And that's what happened. The prize was shared. What do you suppose those people working for this young man thought about him?

As the years passed, Dick's unselfishness rubbed off on other areas of his life. He was active in community affairs. He was a leader in his social circles. Everybody who knew him saw what a fine man he was, and everyone wanted to be his friend. Customers wanted to buy from him. His superiors recognized his outstanding performance. They saw how much business he was bringing into the firm. In time, he was promoted. The pattern continued. It was an unbroken story of service and success, and his promotions continued, along with his firm's sales and earnings growth. He rose in his organization to the top, retiring as a full partner and chair of the western region.

8
Why Care About Feelings?

THINK ABOUT IT. We live in a world of the seen and the unseen. Some things are obvious because they are hard, tangible, and measurable. This category includes profit, output, quality, machinery, materials, etc. At the same time, the *not-so-easily seen* exists—emotions, feelings, sentiments, and values like courage, fortitude, patience, kindness, sympathy, love, and beauty. These are every bit as real as the tangible and measurable. Yet, to many minds, they are harder to see and value. A well-developed soul sees and values both the rational and emotional, the tangible and intangible, the overt and covert.

Sadly, many supervisors need to be more well-developed in perceiving and valuing both dimensions. Here's an illustration of what I mean. Years ago, at Anaconda's mining operation in Arizona, I was with the manager of the maintenance department. His workers repaired heavy earthmoving equipment: haulers, scrapers, belly-loaders, etc. I watched the workers go about their tasks, tearing apart the broken machinery, locating problems, getting the right tools and parts, and putting the equipment back together.

As we walked down the building's center aisle, where the work was taking place, he enthusiastically explained his department's function. He mentioned the difficulties he had finding and training competent mechanics. As we walked along, I noticed that the workers appeared to be avoiding their boss. They darted out of his way to dodge eye contact. All the while, this manager explained how his department ran and what was happening with the repairs. Suddenly, he stopped dead in his tracks. He spotted something that needed his attention. He watched momentarily and then walked to a mechanic working on an earthmover. Coming up from behind the mechanic, the manager nudged him aside. He told the workman that the machine's problem was much more severe and significant than the minor difficulty he was fixing. He then explained what needed to be done, and the workman nodded in agreement. Can you imagine how this worker felt?

What I noticed and what the manager noticed were entirely different things. I saw the emotional while he saw the mechanical. The point is that humans see what they value and understand. Part of our world consists of tangible things—what we can touch and measure. Another aspect of our world is the intangible—something we can sense, feel, and experience emotionally. Logical and emotional—these are the two halves of the human experience. Each one is vitally important.

❏❏❏

It's usually a good idea to ask yourself, *How do others see things and feel about them?* It takes a big-minded person to do this, but it's within your control. Here are two examples of being sensitive to feelings.

Richard Clarke, who ran Pacific Gas and Electric at the time, shared the change of perspective he experienced years ago. Clarke was the attorney arguing a rate case before the California State Legislature. He said, "I went up to the legislature with all my empirical data and arguments about how it would be terrible to depart from cost-based rates, where rates would be based on the cost of serving specific customer groups. The hearing room was packed with citizens, lovely little old ladies who could be my grandmother. These fine people just sat there. And they would grimace and grunt when I made my case because they had a need, and they needed a solution to that need. That event underscored the importance of dealing with needs and feelings. Feelings and sensitivities are as much a part of the equation as the intellectual side. This experience drove home that, as a company, we must be caring."

When the manager of a paper mill in Michigan held a meeting to listen to his employee's concerns, he got an earful. What bothered them most was the parking situation. Next to the plant were just a few parking spaces reserved for managers. Employees had to park in the main lot, some distance away, and walk over a bridge to the plant, whereas the managers could drive right up to the building. They told management, "Look, you drive; we walk. Yet we get here a lot earlier than you do." Managers never realized this was bothering the employees. Management changed the parking policy to a first come, first serve basis. Don't you suppose the employees changed their opinions about the managers once they didn't have to pass a "Reserved for Management" sign?

9

Have Deep Respect for People

YOUR EFFECTIVENESS AS a manager depends on your knowledge and skill. But more importantly, it depends on what dominates your heart, how you view others, and how you feel about them. Do you see people as things to be used or as people to be nurtured and respected?

I encountered a situation that revealed this vital lesson during my assignment in Grants, New Mexico. The Anaconda Company had a uranium mining operation there. It was headed by a man named Albert. The first thing I learned was that Albert was highly regarded. The employees loved him. I realized they were drawn to Albert because of his humility and kindness. He wasn't rough with his people; he treated them gently.

I heard stories about workers getting into trouble with the law—maybe drunkenness or minor offenses—and being imprisoned. Albert cared. The sheriff would call Albert late at night, and he'd get out of bed, drive to the jail, and bail out the miscreant.

Albert wasn't overly judgmental of others. Perhaps it was because he knew of his flaws. I suspect he thought of people as people, and no one was better or worse than anyone else. They all mattered. He had a sincere reverence for fellow human beings.

The operation in Grants employed Mexican Americans, Native Americans from the Acoma tribe, and Whites from the state and beyond. Albert was uniformly kind to everyone. He never treated one person or group differently than others. None were preferred or treated in unique ways. There were neither favored classes nor victims to be pampered. Albert respected everyone. And he respected differences in culture. On one occasion, the personnel manager came to Albert with a question—an employee from the Acoma tribe wanted to be reimbursed for a medical expense. He had been treated for some ailment by his tribe's medicine man, who demanded three chickens and a pig. How should the company handle this unusual expense? Albert thought about the situation for a short time. He responded, "Find a way to pay it. The man was cured, wasn't he?"

On another occasion, a woman came into the personnel manager's office to apply for the heavy equipment operator position. The personnel manager asked her, "Why do you want this job?" Her response was clear and convincing. "Because I have a family and no husband. And I need a man-sized paycheck to pay my bills!" The matter was brought to Albert's attention. He answered, "Give her a chance. Let's see what she can do. What do we care if it's a man or a woman operating the equipment?"

Albert was beloved mainly because of what dwelled in his heart. Unlike judgmental sorts who are too quick to condemn, Albert accepted people as they were. He didn't condone bad behavior. But he did revere every individual's personhood, and by so doing, they somehow realized that he loved them.

❑❑❑

An incredible human capacity we all have is the ability to worship ideals—to serve something greater than ourselves and our immediate appetites. This capacity makes religious devotion possible. Of course, we don't actualize this capacity as well or as much as we should. Nonetheless, it's there, waiting to be awakened if we call it into action.

The quality of human life has advanced over many centuries, not merely because of gains in material abundance but also in revering ideals. The logic behind reverence for human ideals rests on the reality that people are not things. Humans are not merely conscious animals who behave as their nature has set them to act; they are self-conscious, too. Our self-consciousness allows us to choose and ask, "Can I do something?" and "Ought I to do it?" Humans can choose to do right instead of wrong, put ideals ahead of immediate wants, and care for others as much as they care for themselves. And most importantly, they can choose how they look upon other humans, how they treat them, and how they allow others to treat them.

> *Western civilization is built on certain ideals. We will advance or decay to the extent that we believe, revere, and live by them. Guide your thoughts and actions by these beliefs and ideals.*
> *Good and evil exist. Some things are right; others are wrong.*
> *Everyone ought to treat others as people, not as things.*
> *We should be concerned as much for the well-being of others as we are for our own.*

10
When You Make a Mistake, Admit It

YOU ARE HUMAN, you made a mistake, and now you wonder what you should do. Let's look at three possible approaches: (1) Refuse to acknowledge your error. That's a bad idea. Cover-ups are dishonest and will be discovered in time. (2) Blame someone else or the situation, saying it wasn't your fault or couldn't be helped. This approach could harm an innocent person. Eventually, the truth will come out. (3) Admit your mistake openly. If you do this, people will see you are honest and human. More importantly, they will realize that you place truth above your ego. They will respect you for that.

I believe a leader's ability to influence followers is only as strong as the trust those employees have for that leader. Ask yourself these questions: Are you prone to trust people mainly concerned with self-importance? Are you inclined to follow those who act as though they have all the answers? In both cases, almost everyone will answer, "No." Why is this? What causes us to trust people who put the truth ahead of themselves?

One answer is that deep down, we realize that truth is a high ideal and deserves respect. We know that people who honor high standards, like respect for truth, are likelier to act honorably than those with other purposes driving their behavior.

One of the most common ways people hold on to self-importance is by refusing to admit their mistakes. It's just not in them to say, "I was wrong." But those around them are rarely fooled; they see through excuses for what they are. Most top-level leaders got to where they are because of the support they've earned from others. These leaders know that the respect they've earned must be re-earned daily. Here's an example.

Douglas Danforth, who headed Westinghouse then, once mentioned, "When I make a mistake, I tell them [board of directors] that I made a mistake. They love it. And they are more supportive of me than if I tried to hide it. And you sleep better! You really do."

It's one thing to admit your mistakes to a boss or coworker. It's quite another thing to admit your mistakes to a subordinate. Tom Page recounted this incident. At a meeting, when he was a senior vice president at Ford Motors, Tom said he gave a report based on data he had collected. His numbers and computations suggested one course of action. Robert McNamara, who ran Ford at the time, challenged Tom. "Are you sure these numbers are right? I can't believe they are." Tom stuck firm. "Yes. They are right." McNamara remained skeptical.

Later, at around ten o'clock that night, Tom's telephone at home rang. It was McNamara. "Tom," he said, "this is Bob. I just finished going over your numbers. They are correct. You were right. See you tomorrow." Here was a boss with one concern—the truth. Tom understood and respected his boss for that.

People know honesty when they see it, and they instinctively admire it. It takes a secure person of remarkable character to invite uncomplimentary opinions. And to do this without harboring ill feelings toward their source is a mark of high-caliber character. Paul Galvin, who founded Motorola, demonstrated this capacity. In running his business, Galvin convinced his associates that he did not consider himself infallible. They learned they could go to him and say, "Your decision yesterday was wrong." He would accept their analysis if the facts they supplied stood the test of his scrutiny. Some recalled Galvin's words: "We're changing. My decision yesterday was wrong." Here was a man who was particularly impatient with those who could not admit their mistakes.

> *Think of people you've known who've made a mistake, who realized their error and then freely admitted it. Guess what? Instead of thinking poorly of them, you admire their honesty and humility. You feel they are trustworthy. These are the leaders people follow willingly.*

11
See Beyond the Obvious

WHILE THERE IS no recording of the following incident, what follows is a reasonably accurate account of what happened to a woman named Jane, forty-three years old. She had been with her company for seven years. Her performance record was outstanding. Jane was interested in a new position in another department that she felt qualified to fill. She made an appointment with the head of human resources for an interview. Here is what went on.

"I'm glad you agreed to see me, Mr. Jackson," Jane said. "I'd like to discuss my work and the new position."

Jackson shuffled papers on his desk as Jane continued. He appeared distracted. "You know," he said, "I'm beginning to think that many people expect to be selected for this position. What makes you think you have what it takes to handle this job?"

Jane was stunned. She could hardly think of what to say next. She felt uncomfortable. She wondered, *Am I imposing on Mr. Jackson's time?* She wanted to stand up and walk out. Instead, she held firm to her aim. She continued, "I've been in my department for five years now, and we've gone through a lot of growth. Many of my ideas are causing things to run smoothly. I think I can continue developing better methods for improving things here. My work record supports what I say."

"You and many other people have experience too," Jackson said. "How familiar are you with the new legislation being proposed? We cannot afford to run afoul of the law. Besides, you've spent all your time here in the office. Can you handle the job of convincing managers in the field to follow our procedures? I don't see anything in your background to convince me you can do that."

Mr. Jackson continued looking through papers on his desk and, without looking up, asked, "Are you that sure of yourself that you know more than the other people in that department?"

Jane bit her tongue, remained silent momentarily, and replied, "I didn't mean to imply that, Mr. Jackson."

"Then, exactly, what did you mean, Jane?"

You've read enough of what happened to form an opinion. You most likely immediately developed a strong, adverse reaction to Mr. Jackson. It's probably something like, "What a jerk!" "How rude!" "He didn't listen," or "How disrespectful!" Such reactions are pretty normal, and understandably so. Mr. Jackson was rude and disrespectful.

Swiftly formed opinions tend to solidify in a person's mind and heart. Once in place, a deeper understanding is unlikely. Trouble comes when we evaluate, judge, and agree or disagree with ideas or behaviors too quickly and impulsively.

To *see* beyond the obvious, you need to *think* beyond the obvious. Start with the attitude that there is more to see and understand than what appears on the surface. How can you do this? The answer is found by asking, "What happened?" and "Why might it have happened the way it did?" Next, ask, "What can be learned from what went on?" Here is an illustration of how a thoughtful mind might look at and analyze the interview situation described above.

What went on and why?

If we have an open mind, we will examine situations from all angles, humbly trying to learn and making ourselves more insightful and wiser.

People have two listening senses—their ears and their eyes. Jane was focused on what was on her mind—her desire for the open position. But she neglected to see how preoccupied Mr. Jackson was as he shuffled papers and seemingly ignored her interest in the job opening. "Hearing" with her eyes might have empowered Jane to take control of the situation and say, "I see that you have something more important to do right now. I'll come back at a better time."

Neither Jane nor Jackson was focused on achieving the purpose of the appointment. Jane was so focused on what she wanted that she got trapped in an ugly situation started by a preoccupied and testy Jackson.

Jackson allowed his immediate concerns to take precedence over the purpose of the interview. He should have been focused on learning Jane's capabilities, interests, untapped talents, ambition, how she might fit and flourish in the new position, and how her abilities could benefit the organization. He should have been concerned with whether Jane would be a good fit and whether this was the right spot for her. Instead of being nasty and challenging her, Jackson would have been better off saying, "I'm glad we can get together. Tell me more about yourself and your accomplishments at your current position." Jackson failed to listen. Lesson: establish a warm, inviting atmosphere and listen—*listen, listen, listen!*

People can surprise you. Their treachery, meanness, or selfishness can astound us. We can also be surprised when they realize what they did was hurtful and mean and admit their misdeeds. Based on this small sample of his behavior, who can honestly say what Jackson is really like? He might think about how he treated Jane and regret his actions. Who knows . . . he might come to her, admit his bad behavior, and apologize.

What lessons might we learn from this incident?

Don't be too hasty to judge others. Judge a person's behavior, but hold off on basing your judgment of the whole person on a small sample or single incident. Beware of this destructive impulse that lurks deep within each of us. It is the tendency to be hyperaware of others' flaws—and delighted when we notice them—so we can feel better about ourselves. Here is what I mean.

Encountering something we disapprove of awakens and stirs us to pronounce judgment. And when we do this, something else happens. We gain a sense of superiority. Our self-righteousness prompts us to condemn the perpetrator(s) involved. We condemn, and usually all too quickly, not just the misdeeds themselves but the person(s) who committed them. We label the person, slander them, call them names, and place them in the category of unredeemable, from which there is no escape. And oh, how good this makes us feel about ourselves.

Labeling a person usually leads to gossiping. Is it reasonable to slander another person? Is gossiping suitable for gossipers themselves? Are we better humans just because we can spot failure in another person?

12
Focus on Creating Value

ART, WHO WORKS for a firm that makes industrial equipment, supervised a team responsible for developing quality-control processes for their company's products. These measures and procedures had to be validated for accuracy. One day, a new project fell on his shoulders. His team was asked to create an entirely different system for a new product. Art's unit had to develop a new quality-control procedure. As the days and weeks passed, Art's team fell further and further behind schedule.

Art said the slow-up was caused by a never-ending stream of demands that kept him from working with team members on this project. But that wasn't the entire story. Art didn't manage his time wisely. He wasted it, and he did not know how or why.

His typical day ran something like this. First, a meeting to clarify the new product's specifications scheduled for 8:30 a.m. had to be delayed because the HR department needed the latest statistics on minority employment. Then, a little bit later, a flare-up occurred between two key employees having a turf dispute. Art had to step in to settle that problem.

By 10:30, Art had taken three phone calls from people demanding information. He asked two of his direct reports to stop what they were working on to track down the needed data. By lunchtime, Art seemed no closer to getting his mind on the QC project than when the workday began. Team members felt it impossible to do much of anything because they needed clarifications on pertinent matters.

It's obvious what's going wrong. Art's unit is busy but barely moving ahead on the new project. Art was exhausted and discouraged by quitting time, as was his team. A never-ending stream of activities gripped Art's unit. People are busy, but they are not producing valuable outcomes. This unit must change its focus from "putting out fires" to achieving clearly defined purposes. How can it be done? The answer is this: do the most important things first and procrastinate the lesser important things.

Suppose Art got together with his team and said, "Beginning today, we will work on, and only on, these key tasks for the first six or seven hours of our day. Then, for the last one or two hours, we'll handle all the emergencies that arise." Don't you suppose his highly talented team would welcome this change?

At the end of each workday, ask yourself two questions: "What got accomplished?" and "Am I spending my time doing what's most important?"

❏❏❏

A production supervisor, Nancy, came away from a time management seminar with a helpful idea: "Know where your time goes and spend it wisely." This idea prompted her to ask, "What value are we getting from how our team members spend their time?" Then she thought, *Three of my people spent four and a half days working on a particular assignment last week. That amounts to thirteen and one-half days of work. If I multiplied that number by the daily pay rate, I'd get a total for what it cost us to perform that assignment. Was it worth it?*

Nancy thought further, prompting another idea: *We spend other resources—supplies, materials, product ingredients, power, machine time, etc. How effectively are we using them? Are we getting adequate value from what we are spending?* We all need to concern ourselves with creating value.

As a manager ought to, Nancy began to think about how to create value. Ideally, we devise plans to achieve more quality and better quality. But more than thinking alone is needed to make improvements. There's the matter of *doing*.

Nancy said, "I realized that if we were ever to become more

productive as a unit, we'd need everyone's efforts. My challenge was to instill productivity and cost awareness in my unit's thinking and working patterns. But how do we do this?"

The answer came to Nancy when she heard about the methods used by a company in Springfield, Missouri. Its management shared production and financial information with all its employees. Everyone working there began to keep score, as they would in a ball game. They loved it. Motivation soared. Quality improved. Productivity rose. This business approach worked because people in our culture are competitive. They like winning. They want to be winners. You can do this with your people, but it will require imagination and lots of time communicating with others. Here is the payoff: employees will think beyond what their jobs involve and work as a team to make their enterprise more successful.

Helpful information for keeping score:
- Production outputs: total volume, total value
- Costs of production: totals, per unit
- Productivity: units per period, per employee
- Waste and rejects: amount, numbers, costs
- Profit and loss measures
- Efficiency measures: outputs/inputs

Invite employees to suggest improvements for lowering costs, boosting productivity, assuring better quality outputs, and using their time better.

13
Promote Quality-Mindedness

QUALITY IS PARTLY a matter of know-how and skills. These can be improved through training and experience. But the pursuit of quality, the *desire* to produce quality, is something else altogether. The urge for quality should be a vital dimension of an organization's culture—deeply ingrained in the minds and hearts of those in the enterprise.

Not long ago, while searching for someone to build a set of doors for the main entrance of a public building, a friend suggested a local firm. I went to see their shop foreman, John Unger, the man who would oversee the project. Plan in hand, I showed him what we had in mind: a reproduction of the existing doors. He studied what I gave him. Then, in a matter-of-fact tone, he said, "I won't let work like that come out of my shop." He explained why. The materials would not withstand the weather; the structural design was defective. The stiles in our design were not wide enough to carry the load. The diamond-shaped panels would lead to unavoidable shrinkage and let in moisture, causing the wood to rot. It was just a bad design all around. He was not about to allow such work to come from his shop. Another method would be needed. Then, he'd take on the job in a way he respected—the right way.

Once, while shopping at a men's store, I saw a sportscoat I liked in my size. I tried it on, and the store owner checked how it looked. "I won't sell this coat to you," he said. Surprised, I asked him, "Why not?" He told me, "It doesn't fit you right, and I won't allow something that doesn't fit a customer properly to go out of my store." I admired his quality standards and frankness.

The elements of a quality-conscious organization are threefold. The first element involves clearly understanding the relationship between quality and the organization's success. Failure is sure to arrive if customers' and clients' expectations are not met.

The second element involves demonstrating how serious the organization is in its quest for quality. Robert Mercer, who headed Goodyear then, told me about his experience in India. After inspecting Goodyear's plant and what was coming off the line, Mercer told the manager, "These tires should never have the Goodyear name on them." Mercer was ready to shut down the entire operation, which he did. The temporary closure lasted until $4 million was spent to replace the faulty, worn-out machinery. With those changes made, the factory returned to producing good quality products. But something more came—a restored pride of the people working there. Employee attitudes toward quality soared.

The third element is employee involvement. People respect what's inspected. And they respect themselves more when the inspection responsibility is in their hands. The founder of Ethan Allen Furniture, Nathan Ancell, told me, "We have six thousand people in our factories making products. And the difference between having a great quality-control program and not having a great quality-control program is the pride people have, where everybody is an inspector of his work. We have found that that's the source of eighty-five percent of our quality, the pride we have been able to instill in our people."

The gut-level urge to pursue quality was captured perfectly by a vice president of manufacturing at Zenith. He told his boss, "I don't get upset when you've got to shut down a plant to meet our standards. When I get upset is when I find some guy who will take his mistakes, pack them in a box, and ship them to our customers."

One enemy of quality-mindedness is *hurriedness*. Poor planning, procrastination, and unrealistic deadlines—these forces lead to last-minute pressures that push quality concerns aside.

Another enemy of quality is lack of respect—lack of respect for quality standards and lack of self-respect. People who define themselves in terms of their capabilities and accomplishments detest sloppiness and second-rate standards. They take pride in being first-rate performers. This ethic is something that managers do to instill in the minds and hearts of those they supervise. A quality-minded culture may be one of the most humane things an organization can provide for employees; it leads to greater self-respect, pride, and tangible results.

> *Make quality-mindedness an ongoing pursuit. Show people the standards of quality work and what they look like. Encourage people to inspect their work. Recognize and reward them for quality performance and improvements.*

14
Make Your Expectations Clear

IMAGINE WORKING FOR someone who hands out assignments without explaining what's expected. Wanting to do a good job, you'd be confused and uncertain about how to proceed. No one wants to work for a person like this. The more clearly a boss explains what a completed assignment should look like, the better people like it and the better they perform. Clear expectations matter.

Imagine this scene in a typical American household. The family is having breakfast. As the father is about to leave for work, he tells his teenage son, "I want the lawn mown by the time I get home from work this evening."

That evening, the father drives home. As he nears the yard, he notices the cut grass, but his son failed to use a grass catcher and a few spots near the shrubs were missed. Entering the driveway, the father sees that the lawn isn't edged, and clippings are on the driveway and walkway. Then, as he nears the garage, the father stops the car abruptly to avoid hitting the lawn mower that hasn't been put away. He walks toward the back door and sees leaves blowing across the backyard. He hears the voices of his son and a neighbor playing football next door. There is a point that needs our attention. The boy and his father did not have the same picture in mind regarding having the lawn mown.

Think of a supervisor who asks a subordinate to perform work. The boss has something in mind, with standards and details that must be met. But what does the employee have in mind? The expectations should be the same for both parties. Having specified goals is an excellent way to achieve this.

To get on the right path, we need to know what we mean by "goal" and what the qualities of a well-crafted goal are. *A goal is a complete description of a future condition we want to see prevail at a particular time.* It is not a statement of the activities to be performed. Instead, it fully identifies what the result should look like.

Many people are action-oriented, which can be a good thing. But this tendency, the desire to do, can lead a person to lose sight of the conditions expected to exist because of all the actions taken. The critical idea is distinguishing between the result (the goal) and the activities (action steps) that produce the result. Consider these illustrations that clarify the difference between activities and descriptions of expected outcomes.

Sales Manager

Activity—have salespeople make calls to potential customers.

Goal—each sales agent will have sold 55,000 units by the end of this fiscal year.

Hotel Housekeepers

Activity—clean rooms that have been used.

Goal—all rooms on the hotel's second floor will be cleaned and ready for new guests per company standards by 2:00 p.m. Guest-ready rooms have fresh towels, clean sheets and bedding, and clean sinks, showers, tubs, toilets, and new soaps. Mirrors should be cleaned, with floors vacuumed, room temperature set, no odors, and literature set in place.

Qualities of a well-written goal

Realistic. Achievable but not impossible.

Specific. The goal describes one desired situation, not several.

Understandable. Written in language and clearly understood terms by those who cause the desired situation to come about.

Measurable. Performance metrics such as units, cost, time, date, etc. Stated in a way that all can tell whether or to what extent the desired situation exists.

At his inaugural address in 1961, President Kennedy announced a goal for the nation. It was specific, clear, and challenging: "First, I believe that this nation should commit itself to achieving the goal, before this decade is out, of landing a man on the moon and returning him safely to the earth."

> *Results-oriented thinking means visualizing a desired set of conditions you want to exist in the future. When you do this, you can communicate what you expect from your reports. They will view you as clear-minded, fair, and reasonable—and they will perform better, too.*

15

The Motivating Power of Goals

A MAN NAMED Clarence ran a fifteen-person unit known as "the cut-up department" at a forest products company in Montana. These employees produced wood moldings—baseboards, crown molding, door jambs, wainscoting, chair rails, etc. Intrigued that goal setting could impact productivity and motivation, Clarence gathered his unit to discuss the matter. At first, these employees didn't know what to think of all this goal-setting stuff, but they liked Clarence and trusted him.

Clarence considered the range from the best production day to an average day. He tried to think of a challenging target—one not so high that people would say, "It's impossible," but not so low that there would be no challenge. After considering the matter for a few days, Clarence announced a proposed target: 17,000 lineal feet of moldings produced per shift. Everyone bought into this target and went to work trying to reach it. At the end of the first day, his crew was 14 percent below the daily goal. Not good, but not too bad either. The next few days showed improvement. On the last day of the first week, his unit was off the mark by 2.9 percent. The challenge caught on with the employees, inspiring them to work smarter. Then, halfway into the following week, his people surpassed the 17,000 mark by 1.5 percent.

Interest in the work pace shot upward in the following days. Finding better methods became a topic of lunch and break time chatter. People would come to Clarence, asking him, "Do you think we will make our target today?" After a few weeks, the employees began setting goals and implementing productivity improvements. They also started helping each other. If one person was having a bad day or feeling lousy or ill, the others would pick up the slack.

❑❑❑

Once, in California, field bosses of vegetable pickers tried an experiment. They wanted to see if production targets impacted increasing output and reducing boredom. They drove stakes along the rows of vegetables at set distances and tied strips of cloth to the tops of the stakes. They didn't say anything about what they did or order workers to pick a certain amount of these "units" before taking a break. They just set the stakes. Guess what? Productivity went up. Workers felt compelled to finish a section between stakes before stopping for breaks or the day. They kept count of how many units they picked and compared with others. It must have given these workers a sense of accomplishment. Eventually, a group norm developed regarding what a "good day's work" constituted.

Experience shows that goals can have a profound effect on output. This is a *production-oriented* concern. But what about the *human side* of things? What impact do goals have on their feelings, fatigue, and boredom?

Industrial psychologists tell us that psychological fatigue is inversely related to motivation. The higher the motivation is, the longer and harder a person will work. Professor Norman R.F. Maier, University of Michigan, determined that the average individual has a psychological energy supply that is never completely exhausted because of an allocation system that protects it. Given the various activities a person chooses or is required to do, they unconsciously allocate a certain amount of energy depending on the task's importance and priority. We might think of motivation as the energy given to any given activity. The more energy we allocate, the more we are motivated. As the energy is used up, psychological fatigue becomes increasingly felt. This phenomenon helps explain why repetitive tasks that create monotony become boring tasks, receiving a relatively smaller allocation of energy from us. These tasks become fatiguing rather quickly.

I can confirm this explanation of fatigue from personal experience. When I went through boot camp, two instructors led us in calisthenics. I felt more fatigued when one of our instructors led the exercises than when the other one did. I wondered why this could be. Could it be a difference in the pace or number of repetitions? No. I counted and found no difference. Then the answer came to me. One of our leaders—the one I experienced the most fatigue under—simply called out when to start and when to finish. The other leader announced, at the outset, the number of repetitions we would perform.

> *Clearly defined goals improve productivity, reduce boredom, and reduce fatigue, and they provide a measure of satisfaction to workers because they know what they have accomplished. People like to keep score of work output and quality. It empowers them to perform better and feel better about themselves.*

16
Planning for Goal Achievement

THE BERKELEY PIT was one of the Anaconda Company's mines in Butte, Montana. A large, electric-powered shovel was operating at the bottom of this enormous open pit. It scooped up the raw ore and dumped it into waiting trucks that hauled it away. Then came the process of refining the ore into the precious metal—copper. So, imagine the importance of shutting down this giant shovel, tearing it apart, rebuilding it with new parts, and getting it back to digging as soon as possible. That responsibility fell upon Ben, who proved himself capable of dealing with this challenge.

Ben stated, "The whole principle of this project was to encourage everyone involved to work together to reach one goal: the overhaul of the Harnischfeger, Model 2100, a fifteen-yard shovel, in thirty-eight days."

Ben worked out an initial plan using the Gantt chart technique, laying out all the steps on a timeline. The chart showed what needed to be done, how long each step or phase took, when, and in what sequence. Then, Ben gathered his people to enlist their ideas and suggestions. He told me, "I held a meeting with all my bosses and explained the complete plan to them. They were not only very interested, but they also volunteered all the help and cooperation required to make the project succeed. Next, I called in the men working on this project and explained the plan's details to them. I told them that if they had questions or needed further information, do not hesitate to talk it over.

It was quite surprising how the men took to this. When a question was raised, they came in, and we discussed it. As the project continued, we plotted the work as it was completed. Progress was reported to the men periodically, and meetings were held to discuss problems."

The results of Ben's approach were fantastic. In the past, the average downtime for overhauling this type of shovel had been sixty days. Ben's initial plan cut that time to thirty-eight days. Amazingly, his people beat the goal by eight days, getting the shovel up and running in thirty days. Ben's efforts amounted to hundreds of thousands of dollars in savings.

A well-developed plan has these characteristics:

A clearly stated result—in this case, "The shovel will be completely overhauled and operating in thirty-eight days." Notice that Ben got everyone to agree to this outcome.

A complete, step-by-step statement of all the events that must occur to cause the desired result—this is the heart of the plan. It specifies what must happen and when and in what order. Notice that Ben created a Gantt chart so everyone working on the project could see what they were to do and when. Some steps had to be completed before other actions could begin. This was laid out in a logical framework. Ben smartly involved everyone in the initial plan to hear their ideas. He held meetings with his people so they could help identify and eliminate problems or logical inconsistencies. Ben's plan did not emerge completely formed and flawless. It came about slowly, with many revisions from those who wanted to contribute.

Who will perform each of the steps—Ben created a team. This would be a joint effort, with everyone having some responsibilities. The responsibilities for each phase were clarified, and each responsible partner had the authority to make necessary decisions, obtain needed resources, and keep others fully informed.

Resources needed—tools, equipment, power sources, and special services from outside specialists or vendors were listed and spelled out.

Where each step will be performed—two objects cannot occupy the same space simultaneously. Different actions cannot be performed at the same place at once.

Snags and setbacks that could hinder the plan's execution are considered—what unexpected events might delay, or make impossible, the work? What can be done to prevent possible troubles? Contingency plans were developed.

Flexibility—conditions can change. Unexpected troubles can arise, as can good fortune. Therefore, plans ought to be revised as warranted.

Teamwork—it's vitally important in the workplace, especially today. Ben's experience gives us an excellent example of people working together as a team. There are two dimensions to consider: the rational and the emotional.

The Rational Elements
1. Clear goals—discussed and agreed upon by all.
2. People had roles to play. All people knew their parts.
3. Changes to the plans were made when necessary.
4. People were kept updated, and everyone was included.

The Emotional Elements
1. Each person could feel important.
2. There was a climate of openness; ideas were invited.
3. People listened to each other respectfully.
4. Each person felt valued.

17
Five Ways to Inspire Employees

ONE: SHOW PEOPLE why their work matters.

Charlie Moritz, the board chair of Dun & Bradstreet at the time, told me about this eye-opening experience. It occurred during a question and answer session he held with employees. A young man, who worked in the computer room at one of the company's divisions, seemed to be scared to ask his question. He would put up his hand and then pull it down. Finally, he got up enough courage to speak. He started slowly and cautiously. He began by mentioning his attendance record—probably to show that he was a reliable and steady contributor. He had a good record. He also mentioned how hard he and others worked to produce quality results.

Then, the young man asked, "Where does my work go, and is it important to anybody?" His totally honest question took Charlie aback. He thought to himself, *What an incredibly lonely, horrible existence—to be working and not know where one's work goes and whether it is of value to anybody.* Moritz launched into his answer, starting with the statement, "Everyone is entitled to meaning in their lives, and management should provide that within the work environment." He followed up this talk with policy changes to get every manager and supervisor to show employees what they did at work mattered.

I think this story reveals an important lesson: it is deceptively easy to forget that behind the many abstractions in business—production reports, sales figures, profit and loss statements, etc.—there are human beings who want to matter.

Show employees where their work goes, who relies on it, and why it's essential.

Explain how customers or clients rely on the quality of your people's work.

Two: give credit to those who deserve it.

A friend named Gail told me about a bad experience in her first job right out of college. She was a clerk in the personnel office of a building supply company. Gail had been on the job only a few weeks when Neil, the human resources director, approached her with a particular project. He asked Gail to develop a job bidding procedure for the company.

When a new position that paid more than the existing starting pay rate opened, management felt that those already employed by the company should have the first chance to apply. Neil asked Gail to research the idea and develop policies and procedures for job bidding.

Gail went to work on what was a big assignment. She talked at length with supervisors in the plant, who explained the practical difficulties of carrying out a job bidding procedure. It wasn't as simple as Gail first imagined it would be. She stuck with it, and after several weeks of work, Gail developed a set of policies and procedures that all the supervisors endorsed.

With the details settled, Gail put the program in writing. Next, she composed a cover memo introducing the new procedures to all departments throughout the company. Then, Gail showed her finished work to Neil. He studied it over and said, "Gail, this is wonderful. I want to introduce it tomorrow." And with that, he picked up her memo, crossed out her name, and wrote his in its place. He then told Gail to retype the memo. Can you imagine how she felt?

Credit-grabbers are toxic. They demoralize and demean those who should be recognized for their accomplishments.

In this case, Neil should have issued a memo announcing the new procedure and crediting Gail for her exemplary work.

The supervisors that Gail worked with to create the new procedure knew that she had written it. Did their opinion of Neil change after he claimed the idea was his? What do you think?

Three: show appreciation for jobs done well.
Excellent results are possible whenever a valuable idea gets into a person's head. Claude was a foreman who worked for the Anaconda Company in Butte, Montana. Within a week of completing a course in management skills, Claude came upon a chance to apply an idea that intrigued him: Thorndike's Law of Effect. This principle says that people will repeat behaviors that are reinforced. In simple language, it means that when you recognize good work and compliment it, more good work will follow.

One day, near quitting time, Claude stopped to inspect the work of an underground miner who had done an especially good job timbering. This miner had been with the company for many years and was much older than most other men. Claude took some extra time to look over this man's work. Claude was impressed with what he saw, saying, "That's a very good job." He went on, noticing what was especially good about the completed job. The old miner brightened up. Then something unexpected happened. The old fella got a little choked up and remarked, "That's the first time anyone ever said that. Nobody cared what I did before now."

On the surface, Claude did everything perfectly: He was sincere. He dealt with how the miner saw himself (a competent timber framer who cared about his work, knowing that the safety of coworkers depended on it), and he carefully inspected the completed job. But later that night, Claude thought about the old timer's emotions. They were genuine and deserved respect. Claude began to question his actions and the motives behind them. "Did I apply the Thorndike technique of positive reinforcement for my benefit? Is that all I care about—better work? How did this benefit the miner himself, as a human being? Should managers be concerned with more than just getting good results? Is my job to inspire humans, or is it to train monkeys? This incident changed Claude himself. From then on, he vowed to do a better job dealing with people as they deserve—with dignity. Claude said that after that incident, he started complimenting workers for their accomplishments with higher purposes in mind. His authenticity led to improved motivation and morale.

Respect employees. They are not things that produce; they are human beings.

Four: point out possibilities for better work.

It's human to want to feel appreciated for our contributions. But recognition and expressions of gratitude must be honest and deserved if they are to be taken seriously. What's the best way for managers to inspire subordinates when they see poorly performed work and improvements are needed?

A young man, more in a hurry to complete the project than to build it well, showed the workbench he made to an accomplished craftsman who was more than twice his age. The bench was a bit crude, and in his heart, the young man knew it was. The older man looked the bench over and said, "You can build a better bench than this. I'll send you the plans of the one I built."

Think of that! What the seasoned craftsman told the young man was both accurate and uplifting—*your bench isn't well built, but you, the builder, can make a better one.*

Five: use people for their strengths.

John worked at a mining operation in Arizona. He did excellent work when he was alone. But put him in a group or alongside someone else—and it just didn't work out. He had a way of irritating people. John was smart. He knew his stuff. Given a piece of work to do or a problem that needed solving, John was sure to have a clear and definite idea of how things could best be handled. Things would turn out well if he could do the job alone and work alone. He was highly reliable, never violated company policies, and was trustworthy. He had a mind for things mechanical; perhaps he saw the world in ways others could not see them. John could diagnose the difficulty and fix whatever was broken or not operating perfectly.

Management was sensible in this situation, seeing John for his strengths. Wisely, they created a unique position for him and let him go to work, something he loved doing. John didn't manage anyone directly, but he did have the authority to assign people to specific jobs. And to his credit, John had the good sense to leave them alone. Day after day, John roamed the mining operation—finding, diagnosing, and fixing mechanical problems—with great distinction. His job fit his strengths, and his limitations didn't spoil his performance.

You may come across someone who doesn't "fit in." What do you do? Look for what the person can do for you to help your unit achieve its mission better. Try to match work assignments with people's strengths.

> *Make a point of learning about the strengths and passions of each person who reports to you. Do your best to structure assignments and match their interests and abilities. The idea is this: Find what people like to do and are competent at doing. Structure assignments accordingly.*

18

How Closely Should You Supervise?

IS IT A good idea to closely monitor your employees and tightly control what they do? Or is it better to leave them to do their duties as they see fit? The answer is this: it all depends. It depends on the employees—their experience, know-how, maturity, understanding of quality standards, capacity to solve problems that arise, and ability to get along and cooperate with others. It also depends on the situation—whether the work is routine and repetitive, whether there is a need for close coordination among the various work group members, the level of complexity of the work to be done, the urgency of getting things accomplished on time, and the degree of difficulty in reaching quality standards.

Suppose your workgroup needs to be more experienced and equipped with well-established methods for producing quality output. In this situation, the intelligent approach would be for the leader to watch and train, coordinate activities, and supervise closely. As these employees become more experienced and capable of working independently, the supervisor could ease off and let people do their jobs.

Now consider a different situation: the employees are experienced, mature, knowledgeable, and dedicated to meeting quality and productivity standards. Suppose their work assignments are routine, requiring them to do the same tasks repeatedly. This situation would call for a hands-off, leave-them-alone style of supervision.

When my friend Tom Idinopulos was a teenager, he was hired to wash dishes at the Bohemian Restaurant in downtown Portland, Oregon, near where he lived. Tom worked under the constant and careful direction of the restaurant owner, George O'Neil. At lunchtime, O'Neil's restaurant was filled with diners who munched on scrumptious breadsticks and topped off their meals with delicious pastries. George O'Neil served top-quality meals to his customers, giving them excellent service. He had an eye for detail; everything had to be just so, and he was constantly watching that it was—chairs wiped clean, crumbs swept off counters and floors, and napkins folded carefully.

One day, as Tom scoured bread pans in the bakery's basement, he saw George standing beside him. Even the washing of pans concerned George. He knew that spick-and-span baking pans are one of the keys to quality bakery products. George dipped his hands into the hot, soapy water and took hold of the scrub brush to show Tom how to get into the deepest corners of the pan. George was not about to leave the quality of pots and pans to the haphazard and inexperienced eye of a teenager. His role was to teach each employee how to perform their task at a level that would make his restaurant what he wanted—providing each customer with a first-rate dining experience.

George knew that his restaurant's reputation depended on the totality of seemingly small things—the filling of salt and pepper shakers, the cleanliness of remote corners of each room, and the proper laundering of napkins and tablecloths. George's eyes took in everything, inspecting what was going well. He watched the plates of his customers after they finished their meals. If they liked what he served, it was eaten; he wanted to see clean dishes. He oversaw his cash register, usually ringing up the sale himself. Keeping eaters satisfied with good meals was his business and his passion. He knew that profits came from serving good food in a clean restaurant.

Anyone familiar with running a restaurant will recognize that George O'Neil knew what he was doing. Some employees were experienced, while others were not. Those who needed training, like

Tom, got it; George's keen eyes saw the need. Others, perhaps the experienced servers, were left to do their jobs as they saw fit. All the while, many tiny details cried out for George's attention—pepper shakers might not be on every table, a spill had to be cleaned up, and dirty dishes needed to be bused. These many details didn't escape George's attention. He would attend to some things himself; others, he'd ask one of his employees to tackle. As his employees developed better skills and job habits, George didn't need to watch their activities so tightly. It is worth noting that George kept a tight rein on the cash register, handling it primarily himself but allowing only one or two longtime and thoroughly trusted employees to ring up sales. He wasn't about to let temptation corrupt an otherwise good employee.

General supervision—appropriate when employees are experienced, responsible, and capable of handling problems that typically arise.

Close supervision—appropriate when employees are inexperienced, need training, and dangers exist.

❑❑❑

A large metropolitan hospital once faced a problem with its employees. Complaints came from all directions. Top-level administrators decided that something had to be done. But what? The first step must be to find the problem areas. So, they hired a group of industrial psychologists to conduct a morale survey. Where do you think the morale was highest? Was it with the doctors? No. They felt they were being pulled in too many directions. They complained about long hours, with a never-ending stream of emergencies. Worse still, they thought that the nurses and administrators didn't hold them in high esteem for their medical knowledge.

Was morale among the nurses the highest? No. Not there either. They faced bossy doctors, temperamental patients, and overbearing head nurses.

What about the accounting and record-keeping employees? Morale there was reasonably good. There were demands, but these were not excessive. These employees interacted mostly on work matters.

It wasn't until the industrial psychologists got down to the basement, where the women in the laundry worked, that they found something unexpected. There, morale was the highest in the hospital. Sorting, treating stains, disinfecting, washing, drying, and folding the soiled linens, towels, and uniforms . . . this group worked efficiently. They were not troubled by the noise and heat of industrial washers and dryers. Nobody came to bother them; they worked alongside each other with a common purpose. They set their own pace. They talked with each other, told stories, and shared personal information and news.

Why was morale more positive there? It certainly wasn't the physical conditions. These weren't the nicest surroundings, with all the filth, noise, and heat. It was something else that led to their high morale. It was the social forces in their work group that lifted them daily. They controlled their work pace and who would do what. No outsider was there to look over their shoulders, telling them what to do. They were responsible, mature adults, capable of deciding what needed doing, and they did it.

19

Empower People to Perform

HIGHLY EFFECTIVE MANAGERS have a knack for creating workplaces full of capable people who are self-sufficient and motivated. They do this by providing employees with the tools, training, environment, and freedom they need to take charge. Once employees get a small taste of their self-directed success, they'll blossom, and the unit will thrive.

Here is an illustration of what happens when employees are empowered. I learned it from Fred, who was promoted to plant manager. Fred realized that his new assignment would be challenging for two reasons.

First, Fred's predecessor was a hard-line autocrat of the old school. He had come up through the ranks, worked in every department, and had a thorough technical understanding of all that went on. He kept tabs on everything and everyone. He was not inclined to delegate. He made all the important decisions himself. Under this man's leadership, the plant functioned acceptably well. Decisions were technically correct. He had lots of energy, which he expended by working at a high-level pace and for long hours.

Fred's second challenge was that he didn't have the same degree of technical know-how, leaving him unprepared. Employees were passive, did as little as possible, and had little or no pride in their work.

After taking charge, Fred learned that most employees had but a scant understanding of how their jobs contributed to the plant's success. Few employees knew what their plant produced and how it operated. All they knew was their area of responsibility. As Fred's predecessor saw it, all the employees needed to know was their assigned duties. This approach was not without problems. Efficiency and morale were low and needed improvement. What was Fred to do?

Fred continued to manage the plant similarly—at least until he could figure out how to start delegating responsibility and authority. He moved quickly to prepare the plant's employees for this transition by

1. Orienting and educating all employees about the purposes of the plant and how its various units fit together and depend on one another. He organized plant tours, which gave employees a better understanding of why their work mattered. He established priorities and set goals for employees. This enabled everyone to feel a part of something worthwhile.
2. Developing each person's pride in their work. Supervisors would now praise good performance and stress the value of worker contributions.
3. Encouraging subordinates to make decisions instead of the boss. Whenever subordinates came to him, as they had grown accustomed to with the previous manager, Fred would ask, "What are your purposes and priorities? What are your options? Which course of action do you think makes the most sense?"

After a year, Fred noticed remarkable improvements—productivity inched upward, there were fewer bottlenecks, better decision-making spurred quality, and the pace of work increased. Most noticeable were the changes in motivation and employee morale. Employees started to feel a sense of pride in what they did. Sloppy work, negative attitudes, tardiness, and absenteeism all declined drastically. The plant was becoming a model of productivity and job satisfaction. Fred continued to involve plant employees in spotting and solving problems, empowering them to think and act independently. They felt better about themselves because their minds and hearts were used to make the plant run better.

Empowerment means putting more responsibility and decision-making power in the hands of employees. This involves having employees (1) understand what the purposes of the organization are—the products or services produced and who the customers or clients are who use them—(2) know what their job duties are and why quality work is essential, and (3) make decisions as they see fit and communicate needed information to those who need to know it.

20
Avoid the Careless and Unthinking

I ONCE SAT with a group of foremen as they exchanged stories. One asked, "What was the dumbest thing you ever saw someone do?" Numerous anecdotes were recounted, but none topped the man who worked in a warehouse. "We had just received several parts orders that needed to be placed in storage bins. I asked a new man to stack them on shelves that ran floor to ceiling. To get the items to the upper shelves, he would need to place them in a basket and hoist it to the right height. A rope tied to the basket ran through a pulley up above. He was to raise the basket filled with parts, climb up the ladder, and unload them on the shelves above. The man proceeded with the assigned task. He loaded the basket with parts and raised it to the correct height for shelving. Then, not knowing what to do with the end of the rope he held, he tied it to his belt and climbed the ladder. Once he got to the top of the ladder, the basket was no longer there. Bewildered, he looked around and then down. There, sitting on the floor, he spotted the loaded basket. So, he climbed down the ladder to get it. But once back down on the ground, the basket wasn't there either. Now he was completely baffled. He looked up, and there it was—high above, dangling from the overhead pulley."

I read about a Prussian general who, long ago, devised a system for determining how his soldiers could best be used. He evaluated them in terms of two dimensions: (1) whether they were bright or dull and

(2) whether they were inclined to be active or lazy. Those who were rated bright and active became his battlefield officers. Those who were rated bright and lazy were placed in staff positions. The dull and lazy became his foot soldiers to be ordered around. But the dull and active ones were seen as dangerous, and he got rid of them.

We must face reality. Some very stupid people are around, and they can be incredibly dangerous. Unaware of and impervious to danger's warnings, these sorts do dumb things that endanger themselves and others. Here is an illustration. Two men who worked for a siding company were sent to a farmhouse to install aluminum siding. Before they could attach siding to one side of the house, removing a thirty-six-foot-tall metal pole CB antenna became necessary. They had done this kind of thing before. It did not occur to them to consider the high-voltage power line nearby. One of the men stood on a metal pick-board between two ladders. He unfastened the antenna at the top of the house. Standing on the ground, the other man took the antenna to lay it down. It fell incorrectly, making electrical contact with a 7,200-volt power transmission line, thirty feet from the house and twenty-three feet above the ground. The man on the ground with the antenna received a fatal shock, and the other employee on the metal pick received a minor shock.

The self-preservation urge is easily overcome by the failure to think. Here is another example. A man working on a construction site wanted to get from point A to point B. He didn't consider the danger of the path he was about to take. As a result, he was crushed to death by the backhoe when he tried to walk between it and a concrete wall. Because the victim approached the backhoe from the operator's blind side, he was overlooked. When the operator swung the backhoe around, its superstructure (the section of the backhoe containing the engine positioned behind the operator) hit the victim, crushing him against the concrete wall.

Danger is like a coiled snake ready to strike. Sensitive supervisors are always looking for unthinking workers who might ignore the apparent possibilities of risk and harm. We all know that gasoline can be a hazard if not handled carefully. It needs only a tiny spark to ignite it. Matches are not the sole source of sparks. A newspaper article once documented a laborer who caused his death when cutting a gasoline storage tank with a portable power saw. It exploded. This man worked for a company that specialized in installing, removing, and junking gasoline pumps and underground tanks. The worker had experience using power saws and handling scrap metal. He failed to adequately purge the tank and test for vapors before cutting. Vapors remained in the 3,000-gallon tank, which was as dangerous as the liquid gasoline it previously held. The explosion propelled the worker nearly fifteen feet from the tank and into another one.

> *If you encounter "stupid," beware. For everyone's sake, do whatever you can to rid your unit of these yahoos. These individuals say, "Hey, guys, watch this!" a few minutes before someone else must dial 911.*

21
Safety Practices That Work

ACCIDENTS HAPPEN DAILY, and the results are costly. The National Safety Council reports that almost 5,000 people die in our country each year from workplace accidents. And tens of thousands of other injuries occur all too frequently. In monetary terms, the overall cost of accidents in the US each year is $160 billion. These are the statistics. But behind these cold numbers and dollar signs lies something greater. It's the human costs—the pain and suffering of those whose lives are shattered and permanently altered. What can managers do to reduce accidents?

An excellent place to start is with the cause of accidents. What conditions lead to accidents? Safety experts identify three primary causes: unsafe behaviors, unsafe equipment, and freak events. Unsafe behaviors involve people doing dumb things, which are common when minds become distracted by tedious, unpleasant, or difficult work. In such circumstances, people seek escape. They become careless as they try to hurry through the difficult task. Is it any wonder that these conditions cause people to daydream? Consider the situation my friend, Tom, faced years ago.

Uneducated and unskilled, the best work he could find was washing buses at the municipal garage. Dirty from their daily rounds, the buses had to be hosed down, scrubbed clean, rinsed, and wiped dry before being sent out the following day. This part of the job was fun. Summer months are hot, and using a hose is clean and cooling. The part of his job that wasn't fun was changing tires. This was a necessary but complex and dirty aspect of the work. It required patience, muscle power, attention to detail, getting dirty, and dealing with frustration and anger when things didn't go smoothly, which they frequently didn't. During this part of the job, Tom found his thoughts moving away from the dirt, heat, and difficulties at hand. He began to daydream. It's something every normal person does—to slip away from unpleasant work and into more pleasing longings and circumstances. This occurs so naturally that a person scarcely recognizes it is happening. You can easily imagine Tom at the time. He is twenty years old. It is a warm summer's night, and he is wrestling a giant, uncooperative wheel off a bus. The wheel is dirty, heavy, and stuck to the bolts on the bus axle. He must change the tire mounted on it, which will require more muscle power, sweat, and patience. His girlfriend is waiting impatiently for their date. He wants to leave work but knows he cannot do that. Tom can stay where the work is, but his mind wants to wander into the realm of imagination.

At such moments, a person's attention is likely to move away from the difficult and travel to what's more pleasant to think about. But when a person's thoughts are far from the work, humans are most vulnerable to accidents and mistakes. Alert managers know the dangers of daydreaming and its potential to lead to accidents.

Suggestions for overcoming the dangers of daydreaming:

1. Try to have employees work with others, especially late at night, when their work is dangerous, or if they are inexperienced.
2. Watch for boredom. Having variety in employees' work will help.
3. Work pressures and deadlines might be problematic. Don't overburden people.
4. Creating checklists of things to do or steps to take can avoid overlooking the essentials.

Pressures to hurry and meet scheduling timetables and production targets are other causes of accidents. When workers can get their work done more easily and quickly, by ignoring safety procedures, the procedures will often be overlooked. Ear-protective devices are hot or uncomfortable, so they are removed. Goggles fog up easily, so they are taken off. Helmets are a nuisance when climbing around equipment, so they are not always worn. It's quicker to reach across a moving line to unjam a blockage than to shut down the machinery.

Roughly 85 percent of all accidents arise from unsafe behaviors. About 13 percent of accidents are traceable to unsafe equipment. This category includes the absence of protective devices, unsafe machinery, faulty equipment, tripping hazards, etc. Only a small percentage of accidents, about 2 percent, arise from what we label freak occurrences—conditions that no one could foresee or prevent.

Think about what these statistics suggest. If we took a random sample of 1,000 accidents, we'd find that 850 occurred because people acted irresponsibly, doing unsafe things—not wearing eye protection, not shutting off machinery before reaching into harm's way, and so on. We would also find that 130 of the 1,000 accidents occurred because of unsafe equipment. Maybe OSHA regulations and guidelines were overlooked or ignored. Lastly, we would find that 20 of the 1,000 accidents arose from freak events—acts of nature.

Now, let's suppose we could magically change people, causing them to stop doing dumb, unsafe things. Of course, no effort is ever one-hundred-percent effective. So, let's suppose we were only 50 percent successful at getting people to stop their unsafe behaviors. That would eliminate half of the 850 accidents. The total number of casualties would fall by 425. Instead of 1,000 total accidents, there would only be 575. That's still too high, but it's a huge improvement. And the gain would be even greater if unsafe behaviors were reduced by 70 percent, 80 percent, or even 90 percent. You do the math.

This brings up how to encourage people to act safely on the job. One method is to change attitudes—convince people to work safely by promoting safety slogans and displaying posters advocating they "Be safe!" Slogans and signs don't have much of an impact on people.

Another method is to collect safety data—things like the number of shifts worked without an accident—and report these statistics to management or have contests between units competing for the best safety record. The results from this approach have proved disappointing. Lastly, there is the matter of altering behaviors.

How can behaviors be changed? To many minds, the most obvious approach is to police people at work. This means catching them when they act in unsafe ways and shaming, reprimanding, or punishing them. This approach is often tried, and its results are less than desirable. Don't you suppose normal people resent being watched, bossed, and scolded? What a turnoff! So, forget that.

Another method is *behavior reinforcement*, which works well. Instead of external policing and punishing, it relies on self-directed actions by employees. People tend to do what's rewarded and not do what's punished. However, the *reward* method is more effective than the *punishment* method. I cannot vouch for the authenticity of the following story, but it makes sense. A rural town had a problem. Cars were going too fast down the main drag. The town's leaders tried an experiment. For one month, they recorded the percentage of cars exceeding the speed limit and then posted the findings on large signs for drivers to see. Then, for another month, the town posted the percentage of cars abiding by the speed limit. Guess which method worked better at controlling the problem? It was the second approach—where drivers had a chance to improve a desirable result.

I spent a month at Procter and Gamble, working with their safety engineer and his staff, learning how this consumer products company uses *positive reinforcement* to make its workplaces safe. P&G enlists the men and women who work in their plants and facilities, those who stand to gain the most from safety adherence, to take charge of the effort. Regularly, workers survey what's going on and report the numbers and percentages of fellow employees acting in safe ways, such as the percentage of employees wearing protective face coverings, hard hats, etc. By empowering employees to control what happens and keep score themselves, the men and women at P&G's facilities become more motivated to act safely, thus reducing the likelihood of accidents.

When we open our eyes to influences that cause unsafe behaviors, we come face-to-face with two culprits: (1) the desire to be accepted by others in the work group, which leads to going along with the popular mood, and (2) the motivation to meet or surpass production targets that determine pay. Greedy stomachs always get people into trouble. Hungry to earn more money, ordinary people are easily tempted to take risks that lead to costly accidents. To counter dangerous behaviors, top management must establish a culture of "safety first." Frontline leaders need to emphasize this ethic continuously. Ask those who report to you these questions: How would you like to tell a dead or maimed coworker's wife and children, "I am sorry for what happened. We are all to blame. Our urge to produce more and earn a bonus caused us to ignore safety"? Is a fatal accident and shutting down production for an extended time worth the risk?

A humane organization that genuinely values humans will put their well-being ahead of all else. It won't set overly aggressive sales or production targets that tempt people to be dishonest, careless, unsafe, or unkind. Good management demands these standards.

22

How to Orient a New Employee

WITHIN A FEW weeks after completing our company's management course, one of our supervisors, Jim, had a chance to use what he learned about orienting Carl, a new employee. Jim prepared himself for the orientation by reviewing the lesson. This involved two aspects: (1) the person's feelings and (2) what the job involved and how to perform it.

Jim began by thinking about any normal person's concerns when starting a new job—fears and worries that weigh on the new person's mind. Picturing himself in Carl's shoes, several thoughts and feelings came to Jim's mind: *I want to do well. I want to get off to a good start with my new boss. I want to fit in with others. I hope I'll be able to do the job satisfactorily. Might I get hurt? Will the others accept me? What's the workday schedule? When do I take breaks, lunch, and go home for the day?* By imagining how a new employee might feel on their first day, Jim had a better idea of how to encourage Carl and explain the work expectations.

When the day came and Carl showed up, Jim was ready. In the change house, Jim introduced Carl to his coworkers before the shift began. Then, on the way to the jobsite, Jim learned about Carl's background, including his past jobs and interests. Upon arriving at the jobsite, Jim explained what he'd be doing and how the work fit into the overall mission. He emphasized the importance of Carl's work. Jim realized Carl's job was complex. There were too many new things for anyone to learn in one day. It would be stressful. So, Jim tried to reduce Carl's worries by encouraging and creating a climate where he would feel free to ask questions. He enlisted help from experienced employees, asking them to help Carl fit in and perform his job.

Jim realized that orientation is not a onetime event. It's a process that may take several weeks, especially when the work requirements are complex. Jim checked with coworkers about how Carl was fitting in and doing his job. Jim monitored the new employee's progress in the following days to see how well he performed and got along with others. He encouraged quality work, good habits, and positive interactions with others by reinforcing these behaviors with genuine praise.

23
How to Teach Job Skills

A TEAM OF Texas Instruments researchers had an idea they wanted to test. Do people learn faster and better when they are less fearful of failure? These researchers found and later reported in the Harvard Business Review that immediate supervisors could help new employees learn faster and make fewer mistakes by reducing their level of anxiety.

The experimenters did four things to reduce anxiety. (1) They told trainees that their chances to succeed were very good and that they all had what it took to perform the tasks satisfactorily. (2) They told trainees to disregard hall talk, the hazing rumors spread about by veteran employees. One rumor was that over half of all new employees were fired for poor performance, which fueled anxiety. (3) They urged trainees to talk to their superiors and ask questions. And, if they still didn't "get it," keep asking questions. (4) They coached supervisors to listen to and encourage trainees. This step made supervisors seem less threatening, more like "helpers" than "judgers of performance."

These four measures produced amazing results. As anxiety levels went down, learning progress went up. At the end of one month, the experimental group, with lowered anxiety levels, showed superior learning success:

- Training time was cut in half.
- Costs were reduced to one-third of previous levels.
- Absenteeism and tardiness dropped to one-half.
- Waste and rejects fell to one-fifth.
- Overall, training costs were cut by as much as 30 percent.

☐☐☐

Knowing how to train others isn't rocket science, but there's more to it than the logical dimensions alone. There are emotional aspects to practical training. Realize that fear of failure and self-doubt can hobble learning. Worries are natural. *Will I fit in? Will I succeed?*

Here are the steps successful trainers follow.

First, they visualize what the completed task should look like when done correctly and what its desired qualities are.

Second, they specify the steps needed to achieve the desired outcome. They also recognize where things go wrong, what mistakes spoil the job, and how to minimize or prevent them.

Third, they convey their mental images to the learner from the first two steps. They do this by telling, showing, explaining, and inviting questions. They have learners acknowledge what they know and what they don't know. They figure out what the learner is experienced with. They build on what the learner already knows and don't waste time with what is already mastered.

In this stage, astute instructors ask questions that require more than simple "yes" or "no" responses. They don't ask, "Do you know how to operate this kind of machine?" or "Can you reconcile a bank statement?" Wanting to look intelligent or unwilling to admit their deficiencies, many people are tempted to answer these questions in the affirmative. An experienced instructor will seek open-ended answers. They'll say, "Tell me how this machine works" and "Explain what the controls here do."

Fourth, they have the learner perform the steps. They let the learner repeat the actions until they are fully mastered. Successful trainers know there is such a thing as "overexplaining." They give learners enough information to perform the basics adequately, realizing that the finer points will be mastered later with more experience.

Fifth, they follow up and retrain as necessary. Humans are

vulnerable to sloppiness and forgetfulness. Competent supervisors realize that bad habits can develop unnoticed, spoiling performance. So, they warn workers about this possibility. They keep an eye on what learners are doing correctly and compliment them to reinforce good work habits.

Much of the trainer's job involves picking up from where the last lesson ended, determining how much of it is understood, and reviewing where gaps are found. Relearning is normal and ought to be expected and accepted as such.

Lessons are better accepted and mastered when couched in nonpersonal, cause-and-effect terms. Suppose the person you are training has just performed a function improperly, with the predictable bad result. The best way to correct the learner is to (1) get the learner to think and see the connection between their "incorrect" action and the unwanted result and (2) suggest ways to correct the mistake or prevent it from happening again.

24
Improve Capabilities through Coaching

HOW WOULD YOU like to work for a boss with a reputation for developing competent producers? Knowing that you had performed under this manager's direction, others would regard you highly. This is because they know your boss has taught you to see, know, and do more.

Such managers are known to "rub off the rough edges" of their reports, helping them to be better at working alongside others. They teach their employees how to see where problems might arise and how to avoid them or repair mistakes when they do occur. They show people how to work smarter and safer. They explain how and why the organization operates as it does—its culture. They enlarge people's understanding of what customers or clients demand. These sorts of managers also uncover the interests and abilities of their people and arrange assignments so these qualities can be utilized and developed. And, not to be ignored, these managers take pride in and derive satisfaction from the many successes they have had developing people.

Wayne, a close friend, had a successful career managing a group of talented professionals at a state university. I learned that many, if not all, of the men and women who worked for Wayne didn't stay with him for more than five or six years. Employers looking for good people to fill more prominent positions knew Wayne and his record for developing talent. They were eager to hire these people to fill more challenging positions in their organizations. Wayne had a reputation for attracting and developing good people. It was something that pleased him greatly. You might wonder, *How did Wayne enable his people to succeed and move ahead?*

It became apparent that Wayne firmly believed his role was to have his unit perform well and please higher-ups—which it did—and to assist employees with realizing and developing their competencies. While Wayne and his people were building a record of accomplishments, Wayne was also building up the talents and capabilities of his people. He did this by encouraging them to find ways to do their jobs better, make improvements, and identify new services their unit might provide. Whenever one of his staff had suggestions, Wayne would listen. He'd encourage them to try out their idea. Wayne's people loved his openness and the freedom to apply their suggestions. If the idea didn't work out satisfactorily, Wayne would encourage the person to consider improvements. The emphasis was always on making things better—and this included people.

You can do your people a big favor by finding their talent—be it a specific job skill or an interpersonal team-building ability—and encouraging that person to develop it further, finding ways to put it to use. This will boost the person's pride and motivation to become better.

Unlike materials, equipment, production facilities, etc., the human element is expandable. People can grow their knowledge, skills, teamwork abilities, and dedication to excellence. But this sort of growth requires the desire and know-how of their managers to promote that growth.

With each subordinate, ask yourself, *What seeds of possibilities lay dormant in this employee that we could cultivate and put to good use together?* Here are some specific additional steps you can take as you coach others.

Talk with all subordinates regularly. Be careful to give time and attention equitably to avoid favoritism. Frequent communication breaks down barriers between people and promotes trust and joint problem-solving. When a person completes a piece of work, ask, "What would you do differently if you were to do this job again? Why?"

Level with the employee. Be direct and candid. Refer to specific incidents and examples of accomplishments, mistakes, failures, and successes. Stick with simple, direct honesty. Ask, "How do you think your coworker felt when you made that comment at today's meeting? Was it kind or biting? Will it promote better teamwork?"

Identify strengths. View these strengths as assets to be used and developed. Let the employee know that you see and value their strong points. Know that using people for their strengths is critical to your unit's effectiveness. Say, "You appear to have a knack for [identify the ability]. Maybe you'd like to be placed on jobs where that skill can be better utilized and developed."

Suggest better methods without being bossy. Say, "If you do it this way [show it], you'll get a better result." Or ask, "How do you suppose one of our company's customers might feel about the quality of your work on this product?"

Work together. Emphasize a "we" approach. An employee is more likely to accept and follow jointly-made suggestions than ones the boss makes alone. Ask, "What could be done differently to produce a better result?"

Talk to people in helpful ways. "Have you ever considered doing it this way?" (Show them the way.) "The most experienced people I know save time and avoid mistakes by doing the job this way." (Demonstrate the way.)

❏❏❏

In his book *Lines of a Layman*, J.C. Penney offered these words of advice: "Do not primarily train men to work. Train them to serve willingly and intelligently. Train them to study the job, to develop perception of what is to be done, then to turn loose upon it fully their understanding, initiative, and effort. Train them to bring as much of their ability into action as they can reach, deep down in themselves. Encourage them to believe that there is in themselves a mine-pocket full of riches."

25

Correct with Compassion

SOMEWHERE DOWN THE road, you'll need to correct a subordinate for doing something wrong. This can be tricky, and your success in handling the situation depends on how you go about it.

I happened upon a situation at a resort where the manager was correcting a maid for doing something she ought not to have done. I did not intend to eavesdrop, but the bench on which these two people sat was alongside the pathway that led to my room. The manager was a distinguished woman in her fifties. She exuded an aura of self-confidence and authority. She was well-dressed, with a clipboard in hand, and reading glasses were chained around her neck. But how she appeared was not how she spoke to the teary-eyed maid. This manager's tone was soft but firm; it showed empathy and was laced with kindness. The manager told the maid what her mistake was and why it was harmful. She explained what should have been done and why. The message was this: "You are not a bad person; you just made a mistake, and I believe you want to do better now that you know what to do and what not to do."

My opinion of this manager soared; here was a very kind person helping an employee do better. Can you imagine how relieved this maid felt after the counseling? I bet she did all she could to please this kind manager who dealt with her respectfully. And don't think for a minute that the other maids didn't hear about how the manager handled the problem.

❏❏❏

A supervisor, Jim, once told me how he handled a problem that called for discipline. Two of Jim's workers were excessively absent. On the job, they performed well. But they didn't always show up for work. One of the men had been absent 51 out of 305 shifts, or about one day in six. Jim decided to step in and correct the matter.

He first sat down with each man privately and began the interviews by having *them tell him* about the problems leading to being absent. Jim listened; he didn't judge what he heard. He didn't tell the men that their excuses were not valid. He invited the men to express their feelings and, by doing so, conveyed a sincere interest in them.

After expressing their feelings (and on-the-spot made-up excuses) without being judged or challenged, the men were ready to listen to what Jim had to say. And what he told them was probably a surprise. Jim calmly explained the importance of their jobs from the company's perspective and their best interests. He reviewed how and why their work was necessary. Next, he turned to an attention-getting matter—money. Using simple arithmetic, Jim showed each man how much their absences cost them in dollar amounts. They were surprised.

Jim's intervention worked. Seventeen weeks after starting to solve the problem, each man improved. Their absences dropped to two or three days over the following four months. It was not an entire victory for better attendance, but it was an improvement.

❏❏❏

Neglect of self and others is the source of many problems in the workplace. This shows itself in tardiness, absenteeism, carelessness, daydreaming, wasting time, forgetting important details, sloppy work, disrespect, and bad manners. The primary causes of these problems are (1) the person doesn't know any better, (2) the desire for immediate gratification dominates the person's mind and motives (think of the person who stays out late drinking heavily and thereby fails to arrive at a job interview the following day), and (3) the person is oblivious to their surroundings, including others (offensive language, rudeness, disrespect, focusing on one's smartphone, etc.).

These people lack discipline in their lives mainly because they do not respect themselves as humans; they lack dignity. Most likely, parental figures or those in their surroundings did not treat them with respect. These people will best be helped by kind and nurturing methods, much like how Jim handled the men in the case above. Poor performance is not the supervisor's problem so much as it is the employee's deficiency that needs repairing. The supervisor can become a trusted advisor and counselor. The idea behind discipline in these cases is to get people to think about their actions and consequences—to help them mature into more responsible and self-directed people.

26

How Group Norms Affect Behavior

MANY YEARS AGO, Arnold faced a common problem. He was responsible for maintaining and repairing malfunctioning machinery at Anaconda Company's mine south of Tucson, Arizona. Earlier that day, he sent a crew of men out to replace a broken part on an ore hopper. He wanted to check on their progress. I went with him. As we drove to the hopper, one of the men jumped up and began inspecting the broken part. The others stopped talking but remained seated. It was obvious that the crew had been idle, doing nothing productive. Arnold seemed angry, but he held it in check. He asked, "What's going on?"

The men looked at each other briefly, but no one spoke. Arnold asked them, "Why aren't you doing what I sent you here to do?"

One of the crew said, "We were waiting for you to tell us what to do." Arnold looked at him but said nothing.

Then another man spoke up. "We don't have the right parts. What do you want us to do? Besides, we need a larger wrench."

"You"—said Arnold, pointing to one of the men—"go to the supply room and get what you need." Their pickup truck was parked nearby.

The crew got to the work spot, but they sat around and talked instead of getting on with what needed doing. Arnold turned to them and said, "The rest of you start clearing these rocks out of the way." They began tearing apart the broken machinery. Arnold and I got into his truck and drove off.

Some, perhaps many, people might say, "The men sent to repair the broken piston were lazy. They didn't care about their work." This could be the cause of the problem. Maybe the Anaconda Company merely hired the wrong people. Perhaps the selection process was faulty. Another possible cause could be poor supervision. Maybe the supervisor wasn't clever enough to turn passive individuals into highly productive doers.

Odds are, the source of the problem with this "helpless" crew arose not from laziness, selection errors, or inadequate supervision but from something else—the influence a group has on individual behavior. Fitting in, being accepted, and gaining approval from others—these powerful forces affect behavior. We call these forces *group norms.* They are the standards of how members are expected to act—what the approved ways of behaving are and what they are not.

Norms exert considerable influence on people. Why is this? Humans are social creatures—at least most people are—who crave the approval of others to feel good about themselves. You have likely experienced the influence groups have on your behavior. In the story above, this crew arrived at the worksite, got to socializing, enjoyed the nice morning together, and became enticed into friendly chatter; they liked each other. And so, the norm of fitting in by socializing took precedence over their work ethic. Once the foreman appeared and called the crew into action, two workers voiced flimsy excuses that no one took seriously. But there was no sign of overt hostility or grumbling or disrespect to their boss. The group had some autonomy and could have been busy doing what was needed. But it didn't have a lead, influential person to get everyone to replace the broken part.

Group norms are a fact of life. They are as natural as breathing. Because there is no possible way to prevent norms from developing, the intelligent approach is for managers to arrange work and treat others in ways that cause positive norms to develop.

The group's most senior and experienced person is typically looked to for direction. If this person is capable and prone to be productive, you have an asset at hand. Take this person aside and explain what you want to accomplish. "Deputizing" a trusted employee gives that person a mark of prestige and a motive to gain recognition for producing value and status among peers.

Another approach would be to speak to the entire group, specifying what you expect to happen in your absence and what you will think of them if they accomplish the task independently.

27

The Elements of an Effective Group

MY FRIEND, TOM, repaired railroad tracks while working summers as a young man. The work was dirty, difficult, and tiring. It required physical stamina, especially when the July and August sun beat down across the desert-like terrain and temperatures touched the 100-degree mark. As a work crew member, a man is required to show effort, hold up his end, and not "wimp out." Work had to be done right; no shortcuts were permitted because the consequences of a single mistake would be enormous. The chance of a freight or passenger train going off ill-aligned tracks is not slight. So, when tracks wear down from years of use, and nature's elements work to decay and shift roadbeds, work crews must make repairs. This involves removing the old and worn rails and replacing them with new sections. This required digging up roadbeds, tearing out worn or twisted rails, replacing heavy creosote ties, and setting new tracks into the correct position. Driving spikes, moving tons of gravel, lifting, and setting steel rails—these were the duties of the work crew. But these things must not be done carelessly. Tracks had to be aligned precisely; the grade, pitch, and turns must be set accurately for trains to run smoothly and safely across the landscape.

One might think crew members would hate to work under such conditions—the heat, heavy lifting, dirt, and difficulty of getting things right under inhospitable conditions. One might also think that morale would be rock-bottom low. It was just the opposite. With common obstacles and the need to work together, Tom's crew took pride in accomplishing the backbreaking tasks. These young men defeated the boredom and beat the sun's relentless rays by talking to each other. They told stories, exchanged jokes, poked fun at each other, and did things they would not do back on the streets of the towns they came from. Their work was challenging, but these young men felt they were tougher. They were friends, not competitors; they had to be. The camaraderie kept them coming back for more work. They could work more effectively, productively, and happily because they knew each other, shared a common purpose, and fought against common difficulties. At quitting time, they knew they'd return the next day not to dull, dirty, and difficult work but to friends. What drew them back was good humor and being part of something larger than themselves. They counted on it as they counted on their cooperation to get the work done right.

This tightly knit group of workers operated as a team. They were productive, conscientious, disciplined, and dedicated to high standards. Ask yourself, "What led to these positive conditions?" First, the group had capable people who knew the consequences of improper work. Second, each group member was proud to be a part of the group and the work they performed.

And third, the group's norms were consistent with productivity, quality, safety, and cooperation.

Let's consider the elements of an effective group and the conditions that need to exist.

1. The group has a clear purpose that all members know, accept, and want to achieve.
2. Each person has a clearly understood role in the objective. Everyone knows what the work standards are and who does what.
3. Members take pride in being a part of the group.
4. There is openness when airing complaints and suggestions. Members feel free to express their likes and dislikes without fearing what others might think.

5. Team members accept each other as people, regardless of their differences at the time. They can be candid and remain friendly teammates who share a common purpose.

28

Beneath the Surface of Communication

EVERYONE WILL WITNESS or be directly involved in an argument. It doesn't matter what the specifics are; the general patterns of what occurs in such circumstances are similar. Consider the confrontation between Ross, young supervisor, and Kenny, an experienced carpenter. Kenny grew up in a family of builders. Both his father and grandfather were accomplished carpenters. At age fifty-two, Kenny has nearly thirty-five years of building experience. Most of it involved leading framing crews and doing interior finishing carpentry for luxury homes and high-end office complexes. Because the housing market is in recession, Kenny works for a large construction firm. He expects the economy to recover, which may take a year or two. Meanwhile, he takes whatever work he can get.

Ross, Kenny's boss, is twenty-seven years old, has a degree in architecture, and has five years of experience with his firm.

One morning, Kenny spotted what he considered a mistake in the plans. He'd read plans for many years and knew that finding minor errors was not unusual. If one understands basic construction methods and how things are put together, plan errors are easily spotted, and the correct steps are obvious. Kenny proceeded with what he knew to be the conventional way of framing. Ross came by, looked at the plans, and noticed what Kenny was doing. "That isn't what these plans call for," Ross said to Kenny. "Can't you read the blueprints?"

Kenny was offended and shot back, "Yes, I can read. I've been reading them long before you could walk."

"Look you, on this job, we follow the plans as written, not what you feel like doing," said Ross. "And you call yourself an experienced framer. That's a laugh!"

Kenny responded, "I suppose you missed the class on construction basics when you studied architecture in college. Maybe your schoolbooks never covered finding mistakes in plans."

As the conflict escalated, tempers flared. Kenny said things that offended Ross, who returned the verbal jabs in kind. What happened here and why?

We get a better understanding of what goes on in the process of communication by examining three basic dimensions: (1) how each person views themself, (2) how each person views the other person, and (3) how each person views the situation. These three elements go a long way in shaping what gets communicated—the verbal and nonverbal (emotional) messages that people send and receive.

Self-Image

As humans, we are unique; we have the gift of self-consciousness. We are aware of who and what we are. This ability gives us the capacity to (1) choose how we act, (2) visualize how we might or should behave, (3) make choices considering ethical standards, and (4) want others to regard us in ways we prefer to be regarded. Moreover, our self-image influences much of what we are motivated to do and how we do it. Also, it's worth noting that thinking highly of ourselves and being proud of what we can do well is healthy.

How do you suppose Kenny sees himself? An expert carpenter, framer, and plan reader, perhaps? Indeed, he is proud of his past accomplishments. No doubt, he has learned from his many years of practical experience. You can bet that every time he passes by one of the high-end homes he built, he views it as evidence of his carpentry expertise.

How do you suppose Ross views himself? Likely, he sees himself as intelligent and hardworking—enough to have earned a degree in a difficult field, architecture. He's in a management position at a large firm, requiring confidence in his abilities.

How One Views the Other Person

We all form impressions of others. We decide what we think of them. Do we like them? What are their abilities, temperaments, and qualities? Yet, it is deceptively easy to misread another person. All too often, our judgments are based on limited exposure. There is also a hidden inclination to notice weaknesses or flaws in others. There could be a competitive spirit, hoping others will fail. Humans can be cruel and vicious creatures.

Knowing another person takes a long time, especially when they're guarded and not inclined to reveal their knowledge, abilities, experiences, thoughts, feelings, and opinions.

How do you think Kenny sees Ross? A young kid, lacking in experience, with a lot to learn?

What might Ross's view of Kenny be? An uneducated day laborer who needs a paycheck?

How One Views the Situation

How we view a situation and our role shapes what we communicate and how we choose to behave. A person's effectiveness relies heavily on viewing different situations and behaving appropriately. For example, serious business meetings are not the time for joking, especially when higher-ups are present, with urgent matters on their minds.

Both Kenny and Ross view the situation differently. Kenny believes the plan contained a mistake that he can easily correct. Ross sees an underling doing something on his own that's contrary to what is called for in the plans. These different perceptions sparked a confrontation, with accompanying ill feelings and outrage.

When people are offended, they become angry, making it difficult to solve the problem and restore a good work relationship.

Lessons

People are protective of their self-image. They will go to great lengths to defend against attacks. If you want to upset someone or start a fight, demean their self-image. The same thing is true with how a person sees a situation. Aren't we inclined to think there is only one way to see something, even if we are hesitant to admit it?

While we might not like another person or feel their self-image is justified, it's not wise to treat them as we see them. What's the point of picking a fight? Treat the other person as you'd like to be treated. Are you getting paid to get things done or to put others in their proper place as you see fit?

It should be evident that effective communication is primarily a matter of regarding emotions and perceptions. Communicating is a territory with camouflaged dangers. A practical approach minimizes the risks by being sensitive and tender to other people's feelings.

It's smart to observe others' self-images and avoid demeaning them.

29

Harness the Power of Listening

I DIDN'T WITNESS the event I'm about to relate here. Rather, three supervisors were present and heard the whole thing. Their versions were identical. This incident happened to John right after quitting for the day.

Two weeks after completing a training session on active listening, a worker confronted his boss, John. The man was angry—out-of-control angry. He was yelling and cursing and slamming things down on the changeroom floor. In recalling what happened and what went through his mind, John told me, "All I could think to do was what we practiced in our training session on listening: keep your ears open and your mouth shut."

This worker felt he'd been mistreated. As he saw things, the company was to blame, as were his boss, John, and two coworkers in his crew. The man was mad, confused, and demanding one unreasonable thing after another. Remembering the "dos and don'ts" covered in training, John said nothing at first. He sat down with the man and listened. John gave his full attention to the angry man and nodded to show he was listening. John didn't try to explain anything, didn't argue, didn't say, "Calm down," and didn't try to reason with him. He did none of the things that most people are apt to say or do in a situation like this. He just listened. This went on for nearly fifteen or twenty minutes.

After a while, the angry man calmed down. He started to express his complaints and feelings more fully. John sensed that the encounter had reached a *breakthrough opening*, a time when it is appropriate for the listener to say something. But it must be the right thing to say. And the right thing isn't logical explanations or excuses. Nor is it agreeing or disagreeing with the angry man. It is reflecting accurately on the angry person's words and feelings. John said, "What I hear you saying is . . ." and "You feel that the company is treating you horribly." He didn't make excuses for the company, himself, or the coworkers who bothered the man. This phase went on for another eight to ten minutes.

The three supervisors who witnessed the tirade and John's reaction said they sat motionless and dared not speak. Something unexpected happened next. "All of a sudden," they said, "the man stood up and reached out to shake John's hand, which he did. Then the man said, 'You're a pretty good boss. I shouldn't have said all the things I did. Maybe the company isn't so bad after all.' Then the man left the room."

After the angry man had gone, the three supervisors shook John's hand. They were astounded, saying, "You handled that problem beautifully." One of the three said, "I wish I could do what you just did."

How do you explain the turnaround of the angry employee—from near-violent irrationality to calmness and reasonableness? Was he simply an about-to-burst balloon, letting the pressure out? Maybe something like that. But it goes much deeper. Why does the pressure escape? What enables a person's anger to recede? To answer these questions, consider what's happening when someone listens and shows understanding. The listener neither agrees nor disagrees with what the angry person says. The listener tries to understand how the upset person feels. The key is to remain neutral and nonjudgmental. The listener neither tries to steer the conversation toward reason nor give advice. Listening and understanding how the other person feels causes the forces that dominate their emotional state to release their hold on that person. This allows the urge to fight, express anger, and stay mad to subside and fade away. The barrier to communication is the tendency to judge and agree or disagree. The gateway is to listen to the other person's feelings.

Perhaps this children's story, from Aesop's *The North Wind and the Sun*, will help get the point across better. Once upon a time, the North Wind and the Sun argued about which was mightier. Each offered one piece of evidence after another to support their claims of superiority. Finally, they hit upon an idea. They'd have a contest that would settle the matter. They looked down upon the earth and saw a man walking along a road. It was a cool fall day. He wore a hat, scarf, and coat. The Sun challenged the North Wind. Which one of them could get the coat off the traveler? The North Wind went first, blowing icy bursts of air down upon him. But the colder the wind got and the faster it came, the tighter the man pulled his coat around himself. The North Wind blew—harder and harder, then colder and colder, but to no avail. Out of breath, the North Wind quit. Now the Sun would try. The wind stopped, and temperatures started to rise. The traveler removed his scarf and loosened his coat buttons. The Sun kept shining. The man didn't need to defend himself against the cold. He removed his coat.

30

How to Be a Good Listener

ONE OF THE most valuable qualities a manager can develop is the ability to listen, particularly to feelings. Listening shows respect and genuine concern for what's on another person's mind and in their heart. Good listeners care about how the other person feels and thinks. And they accept that the other person experiences events as they say they do. Good listening is not agreeing or disagreeing with what is said. It's just accepting that the other person feels and thinks as they say they do. Consider these suggestions:

1. Set up a "listening post"—a quiet place free of interruptions like the phone, passersby, and emergencies.
2. Put away papers or other things that beg for your attention. These can wait.
3. Expect pauses and periods of silence where the person says nothing. Realize that the person might be reticent, fearing what you might think. Do not prod the person to speak. Remain attentive.
4. Expect confused, disjointed ramblings. The person you are listening to may be emotional, confused, and finding it hard to express what's inside. The person may fear that you will be judgmental, so remain neutral.
5. Don't play FBI. Don't suspiciously question or try to get facts that you think matter.
6. Do not agree with what the person says. Do not disagree. Just listen.

7. You are not Dear Abby. You aren't there to advise—just listen.
8. Listen for feelings. Accept the person's feelings as real because, to that person, they are real. (Aren't we all entitled to feel as we do, to have our thoughts and opinions?) If the speaker expresses a feeling, say, "I hear you say that you feel . . ."
9. Show that you are interested in hearing what's on the speaker's mind by saying things like, "Uh-huh," "I see," and "Go on."
10. Smile, fold your hands, lean forward, and nod. Use body language to express your sincere interest. Remember, your job is to show that you accept their feelings.

31

Meet the Challenge of Change

A NEW PIECE of equipment is installed to boost productivity and improve quality. Some people will feel threatened, while others welcome it. A change in hiring procedures is ordered by top management. Some people endorse it, while others say it is unreasonable and unfair. A new person joins a workgroup. Some of the coworkers will be supportive, while others will be negative. In situations like these and countless others, the acts of change can sow seeds of discord, whereby mere differences of opinion morph into destructive actions.

One of the most valuable skills any manager can acquire is introducing and implementing change successfully. Everywhere one looks, change is taking place. Markets, regulations, technologies, organizational policies, competitors, consumer expectations, etc., are marked by change. To maintain their relevance and competitive advantage, organizations must change and adapt to new circumstances—or remain unaltered, whereby they grow irrelevant and die. Is it any wonder that managers from the front line to the executive suites of any organization face the challenge of change?

To help us better understand what makes change a challenge, we'll consider what's involved from two perspectives: (1) the logical, rational, and (2) the human, emotional. Each dimension of the challenge needs thoughtful and skillful attention to make the desired improvements work. The key to successful change-making is balance. This means giving adequate thought and sensitive attention to the rational and emotional. Carefully made plans need to be in place to address each aspect.

Consider what's involved from both perspectives—the logical and emotional.

The Logical, Rational Perspective

- Different manufacturing processes
- Different customer expectations that the firm must satisfy with new services
- Changes in organization structure, perhaps a new unit entirely
- Changes in work assignments and reporting relationships
- Different technologies to be mastered and applied
- Timing: when each aspect of the proposed change needs to be implemented

The Human, Emotional Perspective

- Employees worry they might not be able to learn new processes
- People's status might be diminished because of different reporting relationships
- Working relationships and comfortable routines may alter
- Social relationships might end
- New hires might challenge or threaten the status of current employees
- Changes in compensation policies threaten people's sense of security

Humans do not always act in their best interests. They can sometimes be irrational, hostile, disruptive, and troublesome. They are known to resist change, even changes that hold possibilities for many positive things: better pay, improved working conditions, advancements in new technologies, and improved skills. It would be a mistake to attribute these negative responses to change by concluding that it is simply human nature to resist change. There are other reasons to consider.

We have all witnessed resistance to change. There are plenty of examples of sabotage aimed at slowing it down or stopping it altogether. Even minor changes with obvious benefits are subject to resistance. But is this resistance inherent in our nature? Is it in our DNA? The answer is "No." Most people resist change for what they feel are good reasons: their status is being threatened, they fear they might fail to learn new technologies or methods, they don't like to lose the comradery of established groups, they like their current boss and don't want to work for someone else, the list goes on. Here are ten guidelines that successful managers use to lead followers through the challenge of change.

1. Earn the trust of those you supervise by being fair and evenhanded. See that everyone hears what's happening in and around your unit, not just a select few.
2. Keep employees informed and up-to-date on what's happening in your organization—discuss why change may be on the horizon and what it might entail. Realize that most everyone will accept changes if they understand the need for change and have a say.
3. Have an open-door policy. Welcome people's thoughts. Listen.
4. Involve people in the change, even in small ways. Make it possible for everyone to participate—in the early phase discussions, timing and implementation, and ongoing improvement needed to make it successful.
5. Announce the change as early as possible. Get people ready for it. Warn them of trouble spots that might arise.
6. Make the change in steps, one at a time. It's easier and less threatening when steps are small and taken gradually. Have employees mark the progress of the change, what's been accomplished, and what remains to be done.
7. Draw off fears, resentments, and hostilities by welcoming their expression. Listen to what people say as they vent their emotions.

Show that you understand and care about their feelings.
8. Encourage employees to have group meetings to discuss the change and what they like and dislike.
9. Keep your fears and hostilities in check as much as possible, or else you could end up leading a revolt of some kind.
10. Rumors are usually upsetting and destructive, especially those based on half-truths and outright misinformation. If you hear gossip (be it accurate or inaccurate information), bring it up for open discussion.

32

Be the Boss You'd Like to Work For

THE TITLE OF this chapter presents some questions. What does an ideal boss look like? What are the distinguishing qualities of this person? How can I transform myself into this kind of manager? Can I change myself from what I am now to become something better?

Many people earnestly try to improve themselves, and some do a good job of it. Emulate the qualities and behaviors of a good boss.

Honest and Trustworthy
They speak the truth; they never deceive.

Accepting Other's Ideas
They listen respectfully to what others think and say.

Clear Expectations
They make work expectations clear and understandable.

Good Listener
They have an open door and open ears.

Fair and Evenhanded
No favorites; everyone is treated equally and justly. They don't try to be friends with those who report to them.

Recognize Efforts and Accomplishments!
They give credit to those who deserve it.

Care About People
They make employees feel needed and appreciated.

Decisive
They make decisions when decisions are needed.

Inclusive
They respect and include all persons.

Humility
They are not aloof with bloated egos. They are not credit grabbers.

Kind
They never gossip or badmouth others. They are never mean or hurtful.

While this list of virtues contains many admirable traits, it cannot achieve what's needed—changes in the person's temperament and everyday behavior. Something greater than a laundry list of qualities that employees believe make for a good boss is needed. If a person is to change, that person must *want* to change and want it badly enough to do all the difficult things change demands. More importantly, it must be authentic. If it exists merely to get something—praise, promotion, popularity, more money—then, at most, that's all that will ever be gotten.

As one traces to its source to find the determining elements of an exemplary boss, we are led back into the inner chambers of the human heart, where we find three dominating desires: (1) to serve worthy causes and advance high ideals, (2) to become one's best because the world needs us at our best, and (3) to bring out the best in others.

Serve worthy causes and honor high ideals.
Product quality, productivity, customer service, profitability, good working conditions—these are worthy ends. A service-oriented manager isn't self-centered but authentically concerned about achieving admirable purposes. Service-mindedness makes a leader an attractive human being, one who inspires followers. A service-focused work environment encourages people to concentrate on doing those things that make the difference between "good enough" and great.

See yourself as you are.
An excellent first step to becoming your best is acknowledging who you are, flaws included. When Oliver Cromwell (1599-1658), Lord Protector of England, Scotland, and Ireland, sat for his portrait, he insisted the artist paint him as he was, warts and all. That's honesty! Examine your attitudes and actions. Try to see them from the viewpoints of others. It is also helpful to inspect those admirable and reprehensible forces that control your choices and shape who you are now. But take heart. Think of yourself as a work in progress. Although you may think, *I ought not to be the way I am*, it is also true that you need not stay the way you are. You can change.

Bring out the best in others.
Suppose we lived in a world where our peers said, "I know something good about you." What if you were to treat others this way, too? You can. It starts with knowing something about those around you, particularly the men and women you manage. What do you know about their hopes, talents, dreams, and passions? When you see others in terms of what they might become, they might glimpse that too—and grow into people they were created to become. Then, years later, they might say, "I'm glad that I once worked with you."

About the Author

CHARLES E. WATSON, PhD, professor of management emeritus at Miami University, is the author of eight books on management, including the best-selling classic *Management Development Through Training*. He taught at the University of Illinois and held professorships at Temple, Miami, and Deakin University (Australia). He was the training manager for Anaconda and worked on a safety management project at Procter & Gamble. Dr. Watson has extensive experience designing and conducting seminars for supervisory, middle, and top management personnel for numerous businesses and organizations, including Anaconda, Sun Oil, Armco Steel, Mosler Safe, Copeland, M&T Chemicals, Bank One, as well as library associations, Kentucky Highway Division, Ohio Banker's Association, and the National Paper Trades Association.

Charles Watson has taught managers throughout the United States and abroad for fifty years. He has appeared on radio talk shows and penned op-ed pieces for newspapers, newsletters, and magazines.

Let's Take the Next Step Forward

THIS BOOK PROVIDES readers with an awareness and understanding of effective management practices. Yet, two more steps remain on your path to better performance: gut-level acceptance and the ability to apply these lessons in the workplace. We can help you and others in your organization reach these higher levels of learning.

Let us work with your organization's training specialists to design, develop, and conduct training sessions to meet the needs of your unique circumstances. This involves setting the know-how and skills of your training personnel to conduct in-house seminars successfully. The key to skill development is through case analysis, role-playing, management games, simulations, and hands-on exercises.

If you'd like to share stories like those here, send them to me. I'd love to hear from you. For further information on training or to share your experiences, email me at frontlinemanagementexcellence@gmail.com.

Visit my website:
Frontlinemanagementexcellence.weebly.com

www.ingramcontent.com/pod-product-compliance
Lightning Source LLC
LaVergne TN
LVHW041531070526
838199LV00046B/1610